Hollyweird

Hollyweird

compiled by

Aubrey Malone

☆ ☆ ☆

Michael O'Mara Books Limited

First published in 1995 by
Michael O'Mara Books Limited
9 Lion Yard, Tremadoc Road
London SW4 7NQ

Copyright © Aubrey Malone

Designed and typeset by Florencetype Ltd,
Stoodleigh, Devon

A CIP catalogue record of this book is available from the British Library

ISBN 1 85479 721 2

Printed and bound in England by Cox &
Wyman, Reading

Contents

☆ ☆ ☆

Acknowledgments

Thanks to John Boland of the *Evening Press*, for originally mooting this idea, and to Ken Finlay of *TV Week* for running many of these pieces. Also thanks to Margot Davis of *Modern Woman* and Dan Buckley of the *Cork Examiner*.

Biographical Note

Aubrey Malone was born in the West of Ireland in 1953. He has been a movie critic with various newspapers and magazines since the seventies. At present he lives in Dublin, working as a freelance journalist.

You want to hear about insanity? I was found running naked through the jungles of Mexico. At the Mexico City airport I decided I was in the middle of a movie and walked out on the wing on take-off. My body, my liver – okay, my mind – *went*.

Dennis Hopper

Introduction

Most of the celebs featured in this book live in gilded cages – albeit of their own making. To this extent, they're just as much prisoners of their celebrity status as masters (or mistresses) of their collective destinies. Many of them are geniuses, some are poseurs and some pains in the butt. What they all seem to have in common is a penchant for the idiosyncratic, which is probably as much a function of their chosen profession as anything else.

Actors like dressing up. They like putting on accents, striking controversial poses and attitudes, mimicking the cockamamie. They like to escape the drab mundanities the rest of us epitomize. Whether they sometimes pay too high a price is beside the point. All we can say for certain is that they're different from the rest of us. They're up there and we aren't. For better and/or for worse.

In his honest-to-a-fault autobiography Tony Curtis (who should know) tells us that there's nothing extraordinary about famous people. 'The only extraordinary thing about any of us,' says the latterday Prospero, 'was that we were thirty-five feet tall on the screen of some movie theatre. We're all ordinary people made extraordinary by our fame, not by our personal integrity or frustrations or any other qualities that people want to give us.'

One thing's for sure: if you succeed in negotiating the

☆ first ground-breaking step onto that quirky carousel,
☆ even for Andy Warhol's forgettable fifteen minutes,
☆ there ain't no easy way off. Which is why it's so much
fun casting oneself in the role of a Keyhole Kate and
spying on these overgrown children as they rhapsodize
about the agonies and ecstasies of that treacherous
Xanadu.

I think I was about three years old when I first sat on
my father's knee in the Estoria Cinema in County
Mayo, Ireland, to watch Errol Flynn (or Tony Curtis)
swash a buckle, or John Wayne ride over the hill in
the final reel to save the good guys from the bad
guys. Things have changed a bit since then, because
there aren't really good or bad guys any more. But
Hollywood, be it the place where reality becomes fantasy or dream nightmare, is still the thing that draws us
in off rain-soaked streets looking for a celluloid fix,
and to this extent even its greatest sins are forgiveable.
And, with respect to Mr Curtis, its most ordinary
denizens extraordinary.

Aubrey Malone

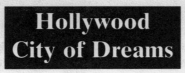

Hollywood
City of Dreams

☆ ☆ ☆

Strip off the phony tinsel of Hollywood and you'll find the real tinsel underneath.
Oscar Levant

Hollywood is a place where people from Iowa mistake each other for stars.
Fred Allen

Los Angeles is a city with the personality of a paper cup.
Raymond Chandler

I believe God felt sorry for actors, so He created Hollywood to give them a place in the sun and a swimming pool.
Sir Cedric Hardwicke

I came to Hollywood with one suit and everyone said I was a bum. Twenty years later Marlon Brando came out with only one shirt and the town drooled over him. That shows how much Hollywood has progressed.
Humphrey Bogart

That 'King' stuff is pure bullshit. I eat and sleep and go to the bathroom like everyone else. There's no special light that shines inside me and makes me a star. I'm just a lucky slob from Ohio who happened to be in the right place at the right time.
Clark Gable

☆ Hollywood is a place where the only thing a person
☆ saves for a rainy day is someone else's umbrella.
☆ *Lynn Bari*

Hollywood is a place that attracts people with holes in
their souls.
Julia Phillips

Movies are so rarely great art, that if we can't appreci-
ate great *trash* we have little reason to be interested.
Pauline Kael

All I ever got from Hollywood was three lousy ex-
husbands.
Ava Gardner

Hollywood is a place where people who used to be a
somebody somewhere else come to be a nobody.
Roseanne

Hollywood is a strange place when you're in trouble;
everyone thinks it's contagious.
Judy Garland

In Hollywood, a girl's virtue is much less important
than her hairdo.
Marilyn Monroe

In LA, even your gynaecologist has a script for you.
Sigourney Weaver

Secrets have always been harder to keep in Hollywood
than youth or marriage.
Gloria Swanson

There were never many loose men in Hollywood, most
of them were either married, going through divorce
. . . or wanted to do your hair.
Doris Day

The only 'ism' Hollywood believes in is plagiarism.
Dorothy Parker

They put your name in a star in the sidewalk on Hollywood
Boulevard. You walk down afterwards and find a pile of
dog manure on it. That tells the whole story, baby.
Lee Marvin

Los Angeles is where you've *got* to be an actor. You've
no choice. You go there or New York. I flipped a coin
about it. It came up New York. So I flipped again.
Harrison Ford

To qualify for a Los Angelean you need 3 things: a
driver's licence, a tennis court and a preference for
snorting cocaine.
Michael Caine

MGM wanted me to play a mother in a TV series, but
insisted on another actress on the grounds that I didn't
look like the motherly type. Shortly afterwards I discovered I was expecting my seventh child.
Jeanne Crain

Hedda Hopper once came to my table in Chasens when
I was having dinner with my husband and said, 'What
the hell are you doing here? I have a headline in the
papers that you've broken up with Don and are in San
Francisco with Glenn Ford. How can you ruin my big
exclusive?'
Hope Lange

☆ I don't want to be called a character actress. That
☆ means you've had it.
☆ *Bette Davis*

Doing a movie is like being pregnant. You've got that
terrible long wait to see if it's ugly.
Carole Burnett

We have a saying in Hollywood: better to have loved
and divorced than never to have had any publicity at all.
Ava Gardner

In Hollywood, brides keep the bouquets and throw
away the groom.
Groucho Marx

California is a great place – if you happen to be an
orange.
Fred Allen

They once announced on US television that I was
dead. When they rang to tell my daughter, she said I
couldn't be, that she was talking to me 12 minutes ago
in Australia. They said, 'No, he's dead. It's just the time
difference.'
Patrick MacNee

In 1940 I had a choice between Hitler and Hollywood.
I preferred Hollywood. Just a little.
Rene Clair

Hollywood: that's the place where the bride tossing
the bouquet is just as likely to be the next one to get
married as the girl who catches it.
Geraldine Page

When Gable left MGM, the only one who said good-bye was the old guy at the gate.
Robert Stack

I never spent too much time in Hollywood. I was always afraid I might end up as one of Hugh Hefner's bunnies.
Liv Ullman

In Hollywood, people have Picasso and Chagalls on the walls of their houses ... but would kill to have lunch with Chuck Norris. That's why you have movies like *Howard the Duck*.
David Steinberg

If you stay away from Hollywood parties you're a snob, but if you go you're an exhibitionist. If you don't talk you're dumb, but if you do you're quarrelsome.
Lana Turner

In 1984 a Montreal movie usher demanded a special honorary Oscar for setting a world record in watching boring movies: he performed the somewhat daunting activity of sitting through Ronald Reagan's *Bedtime for Bonzo* fifty-seven times in succession. He didn't get his wish ... but was presented with his very own personal copy of the movie for his heroic deed.

In 1966 the Golden Turkey Award for the worst performance in a movie went to Tony Bennett for his, er, 'performance' in a movie called, you've guessed it, *The Oscar*.

At the 1974 Academy Awards a streaker appeared on stage. Five years later he was shot to death in his sex accessories shop in San Francisco, after two men with sawn-off shotguns burst in on him. Their takings from the robbery totalled $5 from the till, a used camera and some stock.

Hollywood For Better or Worse

Every time Liz Taylor gets laid, she marries the man.
Nobody ever told her you can do it and remain single.
Lillian Hellman

Nothing happened in our marriage: I named the
waterbed Lake Placid.
Phyllis Diller

I'm the modern, intelligent type of woman – in other
words I can't get a man.
Shelley Winters

One marriage in three ends in divorce – the other two
fight it out to the bitter end.
Lucille Ball

I think husbands and wives should live in separate
houses. If there's enough money, the children should
live in a third.
Cloris Leachman

It's bloody impractical to love, honour and obey. If it
wasn't, you wouldn't have to sign a contract.
Katharine Hepburn

Some of my best leading men have been dogs and horses.
Elizabeth Taylor

I don't know which was the greatest disaster – my career or my wives.
Stewart Granger

The most beautiful women in the world can look like dog s*** on camera. Fortunately for me, it also works the other way round.
Mel Gibson

Would I consider re-marriage? Yes, if I found a man who had $15 million, who would sign over half of it to me . . . and guarantee he'd be dead within the year.
Bette Davis

A wife only lasts for the length of a marriage, but an ex-wife is there for the rest of your life.
Woody Allen

I'm a firm believer in getting married early in the morning. That way, if it doesn't work out, you haven't wasted the whole day.
Mickey Rooney

Three things have helped me go successfully through the ordeals of life: an understanding husband, a good analyst . . . and millions and millions of dollars.
Mary Tyler Moore

The good point about celebrity status is being able to get a table in a restaurant. The bad point is that fans start videotaping me while I'm eating.
Steve Martin

I prefer the bed to myself.
Sarah Miles

☆ Our marriage works because we both carry clubs of
☆ equal sizes.
☆ *Paul Newman*

I want a child very badly. Do you know anybody?
Dianne Wiest

My first marriage was not happy. I chose him because
he knew which wines to order and how to leave his visiting cards.
Jean Seberg

My first marriage doesn't count. I was sixteen. It lasted
one week.
Jill St John

Jack Nicholson and my daughter lived together for
twelve years. That's longer than any of my marriages
lasted.
John Huston

American men are like fifteen-year-old boys with a
hard-on twenty-four hours a day.
Sally Field

Is that what's going to be on my tombstone: he dated
Barbra Streisand and Julia Roberts.
Liam Neeson

I've tried everything except coprophagy and necro-
philia, but I still like kissing the best.
John Waters

To succeed with the opposite sex the best thing is to
tell her you're impotent. She won't be able to wait to
disprove it.
Cary Grant

Men are those creatures with two legs and eight hands. ☆
Jayne Mansfield ☆
☆

The main problem in marriage is that, for a man, sex is a hunger – like eating. And if he can't get to a fancy restaurant, he'll make for a hot-dog stand.
Joan Fontaine

Middle age is the time of life when a man's fantasies revolve around a bank manager saying yes instead of a girl.
Jane Fonda

I know there are nights when I have power, when I could put on something and walk in somewhere and if there's a man who doesn't look at me, it's because he's gay.
Kathleen Turner

A woman can have twenty-five affairs and nobody says anything, but if she has four husbands she's terrible.
Hedy Lamarr

I'd hate to tell you how old I am, but I reached the age of consent about 75,000 consents ago.
Shelley Winters

They say that drinking interferes with your sex life. I figure it's the other way round.
WC Fields

My doctor told my wife that we should enjoy sex every night – now we'll never see each other.
Chevy Chase

☆ There's nothing wrong with making love with the
☆ lights on: just make sure the car door is closed.
☆ *George Burns*

The practice of putting women on pedestals began to
die out when it was discovered they could give better
orders from that position.
Betty Grable

We made civilization to impress our girlfriends. If it
hadn't been for women we'd still be sitting in a cave
eating raw meat.
Orson Welles

If a man does something silly, people say 'Isn't he silly'.
But if a woman does something silly, people say
'Aren't *women* silly'.
Doris Day

Those women who go round saying 'Freedom Now!
Liberty for women! Equality'. Fine. Give them a gun
and send them to Vietnam.
Peter Fonda

A man has to be Joe McCarthy to be called ruthless.
All a woman has to do is put you on 'hold'.
Marlo Thomas

Clark Gable was the kind of guy who, if you said
'Hello, Clark', he was stuck for an answer.
Ava Gardner

Robert Redford has turned almost alarmingly blonde.
He's gone past aluminium, so that he must be pluto-
nium by now. His hair is co-ordinated with his teeth.
Pauline Kael

Jayne Mansfield's idea of dramatic art is knowing how to fill a sweater.
Bette Davis

I have eyes like a bullfrog, a neck like an ostrich and long, limp hair. You just *have* to be good to survive with that kind of equipment.
Bette Davis

The only parts of my original body left are the elbows.
Phyllis Diller

If Robert de Niro gains weight for a role it's called 'artistic dedication': if I do it's called letting yourself go.
Brenda Fricker

The only time a woman really succeeds in changing a man is when he's in nappies.
Natalie Wood

I have bursts of being a lady, but they don't last very long.
Shelley Winters

Nobody but a mother could have loved Bette Davis at the height of her career.
Brian Aherne

Norma Shearer has a face unclouded by thought.
Lillian Hellman

I recently read about a woman who plans to divorce her husband as soon as she can find a way to do it without making him happy!
Arnold Schwarzenegger

☆ The reason Hollywood divorces cost so much is
☆ because they're worth it!
☆ *Johnny Carson*

All men are rats – and those who aren't are boring.
Joan Collins

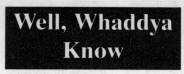

Well, Whaddya Know

☆ ☆ ☆

James Dean used to sign letters 'James Brando-Clift Dean'.

Sean Penn received a dozen death threats during the filming of *Colors* and insisted on wearing a bullet-proof vest during shooting.

Sammy Davis played a truant from school from the age of four, avoiding inspectors by clamping a cigar between his teeth and pretending he was a forty-five-year-old midget.

When Peter O'Toole and Peter Finch were refused a drink in a Bray pub after hours one night they came upon a novel solution to the age-old problem: they bought the bar.

When a psychiatrist asked Robert Mitchum what he liked doing at parties he replied: 'I get drunk, follow the pretty broads, make a fool of myself and stagger home.'

At the beginning of the century, Pennsylvania banned a film because it showed a woman knitting baby clothes.

Al Jolson's 'You ain't heard nothin' yet' was an ad-lib.

☆ Turkey has a ban on people kissing in films.

☆

☆ Shirley Temple was a dollar millionairess before she was ten.

In 1926, Rin Tin Tin was more popular with audiences than stars like Charles Chaplin, Douglas Fairbanks and Rudolph Valentino.

Oliver Hardy played screen villains before he teamed up with Stan Laurel.

Clark Gable originally said, 'Frankly, my dear, I don't care' in *Gone with the Wind*.

Alan Ladd had to stand on orange crates to match the size of his leading ladies.

The poster for *Casablanca* is the bestselling poster of all time.

James Joyce was the manager of the first cinema in Ireland.

When Pope John Paul I died in 1978, Clint Eastwood bought his Mercedes.

To get her to cry in films, directors would tell child star Shirley Temple lies about her pet animals being dead.

If an actor came to movie mogul, Louis B Mayer, with a complaint, Mayer used to cry until the complainant withdrew his gripe.

There isn't a moment in the day when a re-run of *I Love Lucy* isn't showing somewhere in the world.

Fred Astaire's screen test said, 'Can't act, can't sing, slightly bald, can dance a little'.

☆
☆
☆

The script for *Casablanca* was made up as the actors went along. Not even the director, Michael Curtiz, knew whether Bogart would end up with Ingrid Bergman until the film was almost in the can.

When Clark Gable was revealed as wearing no vest in *It Happened One Night*, the sale of underwear plummeted.

Bela Lugosi was buried in his Dracula cape.

Harpo Marx only spoke twice in forty-seven years of showbusiness.

Alfred Hitchcock loved train timetables so much he used to memorize them.

Eddie Murphy holds the dubious honour of having the most recorded swear words in a movie. *Harlem Nights* has 262 expletives.

Helen Keller, who was blind, deaf and dumb, played a pilot in the 1918 version of *Deliverance*.

Liz Taylor and Sophia Loren both appeared as uncredited extras in *Quo Vadis*.

Joan Collins wore a dress to a press conference in 1982, which was made from all the newspaper stories that were written about her that year.

Mae West had her phone number listed in the telephone directory to give her fans better access to her.

☆
☆
☆

James Stewart has kept every hat he wore in films since his first in 1935.

Fidel Castro was once a movie extra.

Errol Flynn was buried with six bottles of whiskey in his coffin.

Two years after his death, James Dean was still receiving fan mail.

In 1983, ET was runner-up for *Time* magazine's Man of the Year Award.

George Hamilton is such a health fanatic he has a private blood bank in his house. (Ironically enough, he played Dracula in the comedy *Love at First Bite*.) He also throws away socks after wearing them only once.

When Bing Crosby was staying at the posh White Sulphur Springs Hotel in Virginia he handwashed all his shirts before sending them to the laundry as he was embarrassed about the staff seeing the dirt.

Howard Hughes never allowed himself to be X-rayed.

There's an Indian movie producer called Bhupati Giri who's blind.

When Julio Iglesias visited LA he was convinced the water was ruining his hair, so he had five gallons of pure filtered water flown in from his Miami home for shampooing it.

WC Fields said he refused to drink water because it was habit-forming.

When director DW Griffith was on location once and ☆
not happy about a shot, he's alleged to have said, ☆
'Could you move those 10,000 horses a little to the ☆
right please.'

Nick Nolte ate real dog food in *Down and Out In Beverly Hills* when he showed the dog how to use the bowl.

Janet Leigh's blood in *Psycho* was really chocolate sauce. And she didn't appear nude in the movie: they used a flesh-coloured moleskin bikini.

The word 'Love' appears in more movie and TV titles than any other.

Joan Collins stopped giving autographs after a piece of paper was shoved under a toilet door for her to sign.

Mia Farrow was rejected for an audition to play one of the von Trapp children in *The Sound of Music*.

On an average day in the US, over three million people go to the movies, whereas double that number of videos are rented out.

Liz Taylor has been on the cover of *Life* magazine eleven times in twenty-five years, which is an all-time record for any individual.

During 1965 and 1966 Raquel Welch was on the cover of 108 magazines.

Ethel Barrymore turned down Winston Churchill's proposal of marriage.

☆ William Holden was best man at the wedding of Nancy
☆ and Ronald Reagan.
☆

Liz Taylor, Marilyn Monroe and Carroll Baker all converted to Judaism at some stage of their lives.

Brooke Shields was a professional model at the age of one; at twelve she played a child prostitute in a movie.

Judy Garland lived in twenty-five houses in Hollywood.

Mae West was forty before she made her film debut, as was Lucille Ball when she appeared first on TV in *I Love Lucy*. (Though the latter had some seventy films behind her at that stage).

Joan Collins received 12,000 fan letters a week when she was playing the superbitch Alexis in *Dynasty*.

1980s' pop sensation Fabian appeared nude in the centrefold of an early 1970s; *Playgirl* magazine.

The RAF called a brand of their inflatable life jackets Mae Wests – and the term appears in dictionaries, a first for any actress.

Marilyn Monroe appeared on the first cover of *Playboy*.

Alice Cooper always performed on stage with his favourite boa constrictor Monty until the latter died after being bitten by a mouse he was eating for breakfast.

David Janssen once had a dream about a coffin being carried out of a Beverly Hills mansion, and when he asked who was in it, was told 'Some actor called Janssen.' Forty-eight hours later he had a massive heart attack and died. He was forty-nine years old. The day afterwards he was carried out in a coffin.

Mack Sennett, of *The Keystone Cops'* fame, could only relax in hot water, where he said he got his best comedy inspiration. He even had a bathtub installed in the centre of his office for this purpose.

Clint Eastwood's first act as Mayor of Carmel, California, was to legalize ice-cream parlours in that town.

Montgomery Clift's ghost is alleged to roam round the Hollywood Roosevelt Hotel, where he stayed when filming *From Here to Eternity*, playing a bugle – as he did in that movie.

Richard Rogers only took five minutes to write the music for 'Bali Hi' in *South Pacific*.

Charles Bronson and Humphrey Bogart made their movie debuts as late as thirty-one; Sidney Greenstreet was sixty-one when he made his in *The Maltese Falcon*.

In 1932 Alan Ladd was an American diving champion.

Because of his involvement in liberal causes, Paul Newman was on Richard Nixon's list of '20 Enemies' in 1972. He was the only actor to appear here, though the FBI had a file on Frank Sinatra that weighed fourteen pounds.

☆ After Pope John Paul I died, Clint Eastwood bought
☆ his Mercedes Benz car. (He had only been pontiff
☆ thirty-four days.)

Eddie Murphy holds the record for the highest number of swear-words in any film: that's 262 in *Harlem Heights* – or one every half minute.

Edward G. Robinson was shot to death in six films between 1931 and 1937.

The only person to speak in Mel Brooks's *Silent Movie* is mime artiste, Marcel Marceau.

When *Gone with the Wind* was premiered in Atlanta Georgia, the governor was so happy he declared the day an official state holiday.

Peter Sellers did Churchill's voice in *The Man Who Never Was*.

India has a larger movie industry than Hollywood.

Napoleon was portrayed in films 177 times between 1897 and 1988.

The horse's head used in *The Godfather* was real.

Walt Disney did Mickey Mouse's voice for the first twenty years of that character's life. (Mel Blanc is the voice behind Daffy Duck, Bugs Bunny, Porky Pig, Sylvester and Tweetie Pie.)

Gone with the Wind was shown in Russia for the first time in 1989.

Peter Sellers was the first male to appear on the cover   ☆
on *Playboy*. In July 1978, John Travolta was the first   ☆
male to be featured on the cover of *McCall's* magazine   ☆
in 100 years.   ☆

Maurice Chevalier learned to speak English in a
German POW camp.

Composer Irving Berlin couldn't read music.

Johnny Mathis once admitted he had eaten monkey
brains during a trip to the Philippines.

The extra who staggers drunkenly up to Judy Garland
to sing 'Melancholy Baby' in *A Star is Born* is no less
than Humphrey Bogart.

Burt Reynolds was so nervous making his footprints in
the cement at Mann's Chinese Theatre that he mis-
spelt his name!

Charlie Chaplin once played a Keystone Cop.

When *Blood Feast* was premiered in 1963, the publicist
issued every member of the press with a paper bag to
be sick into.

WC Fields, who hated Christmas Day almost as much
as he did animals and children, died on that day. So did
Charlie Chaplin.

Joan Collins banned a Beverly Hills dustman from
collecting her rubbish in 1987 after she learned that he
was selling it to fans; she later bought a paper shredder
and hired a private company to remove it.

☆
☆
☆

Bo Derek received 50,000 fan letters a week during the 1980s.

A Las Vegas promoter has booked the showroom of a local hotel for New Year's Eve 1999 for Elvis Presley's 'return concert'. He's already sold ringside tickets . . .

Diane Keaton was the one member of the stage version of *Hair* who refused to go nude.

The original Barbie doll was designed by Zsa Zsa Gabor's sixth husband, Jack Ryan.

Shirley Temple got 135,000 gifts for her eighteenth birthday from adoring fans.

Marilyn Monroe died the day before she was due to give an important press conference in 1962.

Frank Sinatra's mother was killed in a plane crash on the way to see her son perform in LA.

Grace Kelly's mother was never informed her daughter had died, for fear the shock would kill her. (She died in 1990, aged ninety-one).

Because Elizabeth Taylor was a Jewish convert, *Cleopatra* was banned in Egypt.

Elvis Presley told his wife Priscilla that if he ever caught her eating garlic he'd throw her out of the house.

When *The Wizard of Oz* was first released in England it was labelled Adults Only by the censors because of Margaret Hamilton's terrifyingly realistic performance as the Wicked Witch.

The amply-endowed Jane Russell had twin mountain peaks in Alaska named after her.

Judy Garland's last movie was *I Could Go on Singing*.

Joan Crawford was so obsessed with cleanliness that she used to follow guests round her house cleaning everything they touched – especially doorknobs. (When she bought a new house, the first thing she did was to remove all the bathtubs, feeling it was unsanitary to sit in one's dirty bathwater.)

In October 1977, actress Nancy Morgan's husband John Ritter wore his pyjamas onto the movie set in protest at having to work on his honeymoon.

French stage actress Sarah Bernhardt had a wooden leg, and during her early life slept in a coffin.

Sometime Revlon model Lauren Hutton used to raise earthworms as a child, and then sell them.

In 1935 Lucille Ball was fired by RKO studios for lack of ability: a few years later she bought the studios and fired the man who sacked her.

Danny Kaye made his stage debut as a watermelon seed.

Tarzan's yell was made up from a blend of a camel's bleat, a hyena's yowl and a plucked violin.

☆ In *To Have and Have Not*, Lauren Bacall's singing
☆ voice was dubbed by a fourteen-year-old boy . . . called
☆ Andy Williams.

John Wayne once won Lassie in a poker game.

One of the extras in *El Cid*, which was set in the
eleventh century, can be seen to be wearing sunglasses.

When Elvis Presley was in the eighth grade, his music
teacher said he showed little promise as a singer.

The director of Hedy Lamarr's first film, *Ecstacy*, said
that her passionate pelvic movements in that film were
achieved by sticking a pin in her bottom during takes.

Clara Bow was alleged to have had such a voracious
sexual appetite that she made love to the entire
University of California football team in the 1920s.

Christian Slater claims his mind lives 'on the star clos-
est to the Milky Way'.

Daniel Day-Lewis lost thirty pounds for the role of
Gerry Conlon in the much-praised *In the Name of the
Father*. He also, reputedly, switched to a diet of prison
slops, adopted a twenty-four-hour-a-day Belfast
accent, and arranged to be locked in a cell on the
Dublin film set for three days while burly men kicked
at his door, and hurled cold water (and abuse) at him
so he couldn't sleep.

For *The Last of the Mohicans*, Day-Lewis went to a
survival camp in Alabama and learned to live off the
land, tracking and skinning animals, hollowing out
canoes, and making fires from flints.

When Rudolph Valentino died in 1926, several women ☆
committed suicide as a result; in his will he left his wife ☆
one dollar so she couldn't contest it. ☆

Charlie Chaplin once came only third in a Charlie
Chaplin lookalike contest!

Lynn Redgrave won't appear in any movie or stage
show unless a teddy bear is left in the dressing room
for her.

The film *Don Juan*, which was made by Warner
Brothers in 1926, features no less than 191 kisses.

Sophia Loren says she derives great sensual pleasure
from rolling her bare feet over a wooden rolling-pin
while watching TV.

Ursula Andress lost her virginity at sixteen in a photographer's studio. Mick Jagger lost his in a garden
shed at twelve. Shirley McLaine was sixteen and drunk
when it happened in a New York producer's apartment, and Victoria Principal was eighteen in the back
of a blue Chevrolet. For Jerry Hall the moment of
dubious ecstacy occurred in a hayloft at fifteen with a
champion bull-rider.

The menstrual cycles of MGM actresses of yore used
to be carefully plotted on charts so filming schedules
could be planned around them.

Acting . . .

☆ ☆ ☆

When I cry, do you want the tears to run all the way down, or should I stop half-way?
Margaret O'Brien to a director

I do benefits for all religions. I'd hate to blow the here-after on a technicality.
Bob Hope

I pride myself on the fact that my work has no socially redeeming value.
John Waters

I love playing bitches.
Joan Collins

Everybody makes me out to be some kind of macho pig, humping women in the gutter. I do – but I put a pillow under them first.
James Caan

Good original screenplays are almost as rare in Hollywood as virgins.
Raymond Chandler

They're doing things on the screen today that I wouldn't do in bed – if I could.
Bob Hope

All love scenes shot on the set are continued in the ☆
dressing-room after the day's shooting is done. ☆
Without exception. ☆
Alfred Hitchcock

The secret to all comedy writing is: write Jewish and
cast Gentile.
Robert Kaufman

Listening to critics is like letting Muhammad Ali
decide which astronaut goes to the moon.
Robert Duvall

Rex Reed once said my career was more mysterious
than cot death.
Sylvester Stallone

Television is for making one famous, films are for making money, and an actor's proper place is the theatre.
Alan Badel

There are lots of methods of acting. Mine involves a bit
of talent, a glass, and some cracked ice.
John Barrymore

An actor is a guy who, if you ain't talking about him,
he ain't listening.
Marlon Brando

Acting is not a profession for adults.
Laurence Olivier

The most important thing in acting is honesty. Once
you learn to fake that, you're in.
Sam Goldwyn

☆ The chief requisite of an actor is the ability to do noth-
☆ ing well.
☆ *Alfred Hitchcock*

Actors spend their lives doing things people are put in
asylums for.
Jane Fonda

It is best in the theatre to act with confidence no matter how little right you have to it.
Lillian Hellman

I learned two things at RADA. First that I couldn't act:
second that it didn't matter.
Wilfred Hyde White

Every actor in his heart believes everything bad that's
printed about him.
Orson Welles

The physical labours actors have to do wouldn't tax an
embryo.
Neil Simon

Scratch an actor and you'll find an actress.
Dorothy Parker

It is a great help for a man to be in love with himself.
For an actor, however, it is absolutely essential.
Robert Morley

I'm now at the age where I've got to prove that I'm just
as good as I never was.
Rex Harrison

☆
☆
☆

I love acting. It's so much more real than life.
Oscar Wilde

Acting is standing up naked and turning round very slowly.
Rosalind Russell

We used to have actresses trying to become stars; now we have stars trying to become actresses.
Laurence Olivier

Acting is the most minor of gifts and not a very high-class way to earn a living. After all, Shirley Temple could do it at the age of four.
Katharine Hepburn

It's just hustling. Some people are hustling money, some power. I don't put it down. But I resent people putting it up.
Marlon Brando

It's like making love. It's better if your partner is good but still possible if they aren't.
Jeremy Irons

I call it farting about in disguise.
Peter O'Toole

It sounds pompous, but it's the nearest thing I can do to being God. I'm trying to create human beings and so does He.
Rod Steiger

You don't have to be smart to do it. Just look at our last President.
Cher

☆
☆
☆

I do a job. I get paid. I go home.
Maureen Stapleton

Learn your lines, don't bump into the furniture – and in kissing scenes, keep your mouth closed.
Ronald Reagan

If you're in it for any length of time you'll evolve into either a director or a drunk.
Gene Hackman

My mother was against me being an actress until I met Frank Sinatra.
Angie Dickinson

When I was about eight I mentioned to my father that I wanted to do it and he gave me a wallop across the face.
Gretta Scacchi

For an actor, success is simply delayed failure.
Graham Greene

Seventy-five per cent of being successful as an actor is pure luck – the rest is just endurance.
Gene Hackman

Life's what's important. Walking, houses, family. Birth and pain and joy. Acting's just waiting for a custard pie, that's all.
Katharine Hepburn

You say, 'Let's get it done real' – but acting is just one version of the unreal after another.
Jack Nicholson

The art of acting consists in keeping people from coughing. ☆ ☆ ☆
Ralph Richardson

An actor is not quite a human being – but then, who is?
George Sanders

Very good actors never seem to talk about their art. Very bad ones never stop.
John Whiting

Even if Rock Hudson had been healthy when doing *Dynasty*, the scripts would have done him in.
Barbara Stanwyck

My pictures always seem to be filmed in places I can't pronounce.
Roger Moore

The bad thing about being with an actor is that his role tends to stay with him all the time. The good thing about being with an actor is . . . well I can't think of any good thing.
Sally Field

No matter how famous you are, the size of your funeral usually depends on the weather.
Rosemary Clooney

It only goes to prove what they always say: give the public what they want and they'll turn out for it.
Red Skelton on the large turn-out at Harry Cohn's funeral.

☆ Fame is like being pecked to death by a thousand
☆ pigeons.
☆ *Bob Hoskins*

I got my first assignment as a director in 1927. I was
slim, arrogant, intelligent, cocksure, dreamy and irritating. Today I'm no longer slim.
Michael Powell

It's pretty sad when a person has to lose weight to play
Babe Ruth.
John Goodman

I liked myself better when I wasn't me.
Carol Burnett

You could put all the talent I had into one eye, and still
not suffer from impaired vision.
Veronica Lake

My acting range? Left eyebrow raised, right eyebrow
raised.
Roger Moore

I'm no actor, and I have sixty-four films to prove it.
Victor Mature

People think I have an interesting walk. I'm just trying
to hold my stomach in.
Robert Mitchum

There were times when my pants were so thin, I could
sit on a dime and know if it was head or tails.
Spencer Tracy

I was a shy, ugly kid who lived a big fantasy life. I ☆
thought I was an angel from heaven sent to cure polio. ☆
When Dr Salk did it, I was really pissed off. ☆
Cher

I eat when I'm depressed and I eat when I'm happy.
When I can't decide whether I'm depressed or happy,
I make the decision while I'm eating.
Oprah Winfrey

I started out as a lousy actress and I've remained one.
Brigitte Bardot

I'm not very good at being me. That's why I love acting
so much.
Deborah Kerr

I was thrown out of a mental hospital because I
depressed the patients.
Oscar Levant

I was one of fifteen children, and the only contact I had
with my mother was when she took me between her
knees to pull lice out of my head.
Charles Bronson

I used to play a lot of lab assistants. I'd be the guy running in, yelling, 'The place is on fire'. I'd come in, go
out and that was it. I never got shot or died. If that had
happened, I would have gotten more screen time than
average . . . I did a 'Francis The Talking Mule' picture
once.
Clint Eastwood

I got my first part because I could belch on cue.
Charles Bronson

☆ Bunuel cast me in *Viridiana* because he had been
☆ impressed by a previous performance of mine as a
☆ corpse.
Fernando Ray

Their Wicked, Wicked Ways

Is cocaine habit-forming? Of course not. I oughta know – I've been using it for years.
Tallulah Bankhead

Actually it only takes me one drink to get loaded. The trouble is, I don't know if it's the thirteenth or the fourteenth.
George Burns

One thing I regret about the past is the length of it. If I had to live it all over again I'd make the same mistakes – only sooner.
Tallulah Bankhead

The public always expected me to be a playboy, and a decent chap never lets his public down.
Errol Flynn

Exercise? I get it on the golf course. When I see my friends collapse, I run for the paramedics.
Red Skelton

I've been smoking shit for about forty years, but it never got to be a habit with me.
Robert Mitchum

☆ The best research for playing a drunk is being a British
☆ actor for twenty years.
☆ *Michael Caine*

My recipe for happiness? Good health and a bad
memory.
Ingrid Bergman

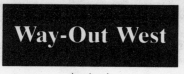

Way-Out West

She was the Madonna of yesteryear. Anyone else who tried to be as outspoken as she would have been ridden out of town, but Mae West accrued for herself a kind of negative, self-trivializing allure. The following are some of her more memorable one-liners:

I used to be Snow White, but I drifted.

Too much of a good thing can be wonderful.

I feel like a million tonight – but one at a time please.

Give a man a free hand and he'll run it all over you.

It's better to be looked over than overlooked.

To err is human, but it feels divine.

When a girl goes wrong, men go right after her.

Is that a gun in your pocket or are you just glad to be here?

Between two evils, I always pick the one I never tried before.

I once had a platoonic relationship with a squadron of soldiers.

It's not the men in my life that counts, it's the life in my men.

I always say, keep a diary and one day it'll keep you.

When I'm good I'm very very good, and when I'm bad I'm even better.

You ought to get out of those wet clothes and into a dry martini.

I've been on more laps than a table napkin.

I don't know a lot about politics, but I'd recognize a good party man if I saw one.

I'd be insulted if a picture I was in didn't get an X-rating.

A little hush money can do a lot of talking.

A curve is the loveliest distance between two points.

Watching the *Rivers* Flow

☆ ☆ ☆

There's invective and invective. And then there's Joan Rivers. She has a tongue like a chainsaw, and then some. This is the kind of heart-warming, feel-good magnanimity you can expect from her if you had her over for the evening:

I have no sex appeal – I have to blindfold my vibrator.

My mother gave me this advice: trust and adore your husband . . . and get as much as you can in your own name.

I was such an ugly baby, the doctor slapped the *afterbirth*.

Nancy Reagan's skin is so tight, when she crosses her legs, her mouth snaps open.

It's so long since I've had sex I can't remember who gets tied up.

An actress is someone with no acting ability who sits around waiting to go on alimony.

I saw Mick Jagger suck an egg out of a chicken. He can play a tuba from both ends.

☆ I told my husband my boobs had gone, my stomach
☆ was gone, I asked him to say something nice about my
☆ legs. 'Blue goes with everything,' he said.

Prince Charles's ears are so big, he could hang-glide across the Falklands.

It was an ideal divorce: she got the kids and he got the maid.

A friend of mine confused her valium and her birth control pills. She had fifteen kids but didn't give a shit.

'Weirdos'

★ ★ ★

Cher

She was born Cherilyn Sarkisian in – would you believe – 1946. She has Armenian, Turkish, French and Cherokee Indian blood coursing through her veins.

Her parents divorced when she was eleven months old. It was eleven years before she saw her father again. When she was eight, her father was sentenced to three years in San Quentin for possession of heroin. At the time of writing, her mother has been married nine times. Three of these were to Cher's father John Sarkisian.

Being married to Greg Allen, she says, was 'like going to Disneyland on acid. You knew you had a good time, but you can't remember what you did.'

She had her first date when she was eleven, lost her virginity at fourteen and slept with Warren Beatty a year later. 'He was technically good,' she allowed, 'but I felt nothing.'

She gets irked when people fulminate against her proclivity for wild living and toy boys. The truth is as follows:
    I don't smoke.
    I don't drink to speak of.
    I don't take drugs at all.
    I take care of my two children.
    I've been married twice, once for eleven years and once for three.
    I don't go out with more than one man at a time . . .
    But do you know what it is . . . I dress strange.

☆
☆   She's dyslexic, but didn't discover it until she was
☆   thirty.

Apropos the rampant rumours about her plastic surgery, she says: 'I had the hair under my arms taken care of. I had an operation to firm up my breasts – and I spend about $1,000 a week to have my toenails, fingernails, eyebrows and hair put into top shape. I'm the female equivalent of a counterfeit $20 bill. But if I want to put my tits on my back, that's my business.

In 1974, feeling herself too dominated by Sonny, she filed for divorce. 'I didn't leave him for another man,' she said afterwards, 'but another woman – me.'

Peter Bogdanovitch, who directed her in *Mask*, spoke of the experience as 'like being in a blender with an alligator'.

'People used to hate me and now they love me,' she said some time ago. 'Not that I give a damn either way.'

Robert Mitchum

His mother was born in Oslo. His father, who was crushed to death by a railway boxcar reversing on him, was of Scots-Irish descent on one side and Blackfoot Indian on the other.

His career as a saxophonist ended when he was sacked from his band after dropping a firecracker into a brass horn. Other pre-acting occupations included circus bareback rider, spy behind the German lines in Belgium, and heavyweight boxer.

His Hollywood debut was in the forty-third *Hopalong Cassidy* film. He appeared in seven more of these afterwards for $100 a week 'plus all the horse manure I could take home'.

He appeared in seventeen films in 1943. Hardly surprisingly, they were all bit parts. He says of this time, 'I was a character actor so I played everything from Chinese laundrymen to midgets, to Irish washerwomen to faggots'. (His sixteenth film was a Laurel and Hardy outing.)

Asked about previous experience at an early screen test, he said: 'I've played two support roles to a dog'.

When people ask him for his autograph he signs it Kirk Douglas.

He's done enough crappy movies in his time, he says, 'to grow more than a few flowers'.

☆
☆
☆

He once defined himself as a whore with a heart of gold.

He thinks about retiring every morning.

He met Marilyn Monroe when she was sixteen and concluded, 'she had no sex appeal whatsoever'.

He was married in a kitchen because 'it was the warmest room in the house'. (It did, however, smell of 'cabbage and a wasted preacher'.)

Asked once how he kept so fit he replied, 'I don't play golf or tennis or do anything remotely resembling exercise. I take my exercise by lying on the grass and looking up at the sky.'

Asked by a newsman if his (long-lasting) marriage was ever in jeopardy he said, 'Every time I went into the studio in the morning.' To which his wife added, 'And every time he didn't shave.'

He spent sixty days in jail for possession of marijuana in 1949. 'It's been the finest vacation I've had in years,' he said afterwards, claiming it cured his insomnia also.

In 1950 he was awarded the Least Co-operative Actor Award by the Hollywood Women's Press Club. He also received 'prominent' mention in several Ten Worst Dressed Americans lists, and a society columnist's Ten Most Undesirable Male Guests List.

His wardrobe for playing Marlowe in *The Big Sleep* consisted, he said, of a suit once worn by Michael Caine and originally by Victor Mature. It hadn't been cleaned since, he added.

One critic described him in *Out of the Past* as being similar to 'Bing Crosby supersaturated with barbiturates'.

He regards acting as a 'ridiculous and humiliating' profession. 'I make faces for the silver screen because I just don't have anything better to do . . . It must be a lot more fun running a country store'. Movie-making he describes as a 'dull, aching euphoria'.

He said in 1991 that he would like to devote the rest of his life to setting up a convalescent home for the rehabilitation of celibate ex-cons.

He has survived in a cut-throat industry, he claims, 'because I work hard and don't take up too much time'.

There are three times in a man's life when it's useless trying to hold him to what he says, he believes: when he's drunk, when he's in love . . . and when he's running for office.

Asked why he was still acting, he replied: 'How else could a no-talent guy like me make this kind of dough? Besides, it keeps me off the streets. The thing I like best about acting is the days off. I'm the oldest whore in the business. I've got the same attitude now as when I started. I haven't changed anything but my underwear.'

His typical fan, he claims, is all warts and terminal dandruff. When one of the above calls to his home, his wife pretends to be the housekeeper and says, 'They're away.'

☆
☆
☆

Zsa Zsa Gabor

She's been married nine times, and says she's had affairs with such as Richard Burton and JFK – but spurned the advances of celebs like Warren Beatty and Elvis Presley.

When she had a fever as a child, her grandmother would cure it by prescribing champagne for her.

Somebody once said to her: 'I've just broken off my engagement to a wonderful man who gave me a beautiful home, lingerie, a mink coat, diamonds, a stove and an expensive car. Now that we're no longer engaged, what should I give back?' And she answered: 'The stove.'

Asked if she believed in large families, she said, 'Oh yes – every woman should have at least three husbands.'

Whenever she has a problem, her solution is: take a bath and wash your hair.

Winston Churchill's son once came to her house to court her, but was dismissed by her maid. When Zsa Zsa asked for an explanation, the maid said, 'I wouldn't want him – and if I wouldn't, why would you?'

If she had met Sean Connery when she was seventeen, she says, they would still be married . . . with ten children.

When she was twelve she kissed the coalman – she hasn't looked back since!

Her husband George Sanders once asked her to seduce a Catholic priest – and she did!

She's not altogether sure if she dreams in Hungarian or English.

She was once asked whom she planned to marry next, and she replied, 'A man who appreciates the finer things in life – diamonds, furs . . . and me.'

Early one morning in her Bel Air mansion she was awakened by a man brandishing a gun. 'This is a stick-up, get up,' he ordered, and she replied, 'Come back later, I'm sleeping.' As he ransacked her cabinets, she pleaded, 'Look, this is America. You're still a young man. If you stop now, you can still become President.'

She believes that if you put a hat on your head, it always means bad news. And that if a mirror breaks, you have to go to Paris, stand on the Pont Alexandre II, and throw the pieces over your shoulder into the Seine, or you'll have bad luck for the rest of your life.

John Huston, who directed her in *Moulin Rouge*, said to his cinematographer on the set of that movie, 'Move in close. If they can see how beautiful she is, they won't notice she can't act.' And to the lady herself: 'Darling, as you know nothing about filming, I'm going to put a heart on the camera, and then you come down the staircase, wiggle that Hungarian ass, and just look into the heart.'

She feels that the blood of Attila the Hun and Genghis Khan courses through her veins.

After Sammy Davis Jr laid his lips on hers on his show on the 1970s, her then husband Joshua Cosdan said to her, with despair in his voice, 'I'll never be able to go

☆
☆
☆

back to Texas now that my wife has been kissed by a darkie.'

Getting divorced because you no longer love a man, she believes, is just as silly as getting married because you *do*.

Men are like fires, she says: they go out when unattended.

She never hated any man enough to give him his diamonds back.

She believes people should marry for love ... and keep on marrying until they find it.

She believes the plural of spouse is spice.

Macho, she feels, doesn't prove mucho.

'If I believed all the things that are written about me,' she said once, 'I'd hate my guts too'.

She married a lawyer once, she said, 'so he can handle the divorce'.

Oscar Levant said she had discovered 'the secret of eternal middle age'.

'I vant a man who is kind and understanding,' she said once. 'Is zat too much to ask of a millionaire?'

The only place men want depth in a woman, she feels, is in her *décolletage*.

Woman's Lib didn't change her sexual behaviour: 'It ☆
wouldn't dare!' ☆
☆

She hasn't known many open marriages 'but quite a few have been ajar'.

A man is incomplete until he's married, she believes . . . and then he's finished.

'I'm a wonderful housekeeper,' she says. 'Every time I get divorced, I keep the house.'

Her views on sex? 'Personally I know nothing about it because I've always been married.'

Here's her botanical guide to men: 'Red roses mean love: an orchid means he's after something.'

☆
☆
☆

Peter Ustinov

He was conceived in Leningrad but born in London. 'Of the actual events surrounding my birth I remember very little,' he says.

He was baptized in the Jordan.

He hardly cried at all as a baby, 'preferring to sublimate all my internal pressures into a kind of patient gurgling'. His shape was 'almost perfectly spherical, causing my parents frequent anxieties as they feared they had left me upside down, and forcing them to enter and re-enter rooms in which I had been left in order to check'.

The facts of life were explained to him at an embarrassingly late stage of his youth. His first reaction was one of 'horrified claustrophobia. I didn't understand how I had survived nine months of incarceration in a belly without a breath of fresh air.'

His father he describes as 'something of a ham'. He once declared he refused to live over seventy, and it was sheer willpower on his part, according to Peter, that caused him to die four hours before his seventieth birthday.

His first play he describes as a 'comedy – farce – melodrama – tragedy'. It involved Chicago gangsters in the English countryside, was fifteen pages long, and had four or five deaths to the page.

He grew a beard for the part of Nero in *Quo Vadis* but MGM didn't think it was real enough so he had to wear a false one!

'If Botticelli were alive today,' he said once, 'he'd be writing for *Vogue*'.

On his first application to enter the US, he described his colour as 'pink'.

Comedy, he feels, is simply a funny way of being serious.

His view of technology is succinct: We used to have lots of questions to which there were no answers. Now, with the computer, there are lots of answers to which we haven't even thought up the questions.

He comes from a pre-permissive age. 'In my day,' he says, 'there were things that were done and things that were not done. And there was even a way of doing things that were not done!'

When he was young he used to fight shy of drinking water when he was made to eat fish, as he fancied that the fish, 'even masticated to a pulp, might miraculously come together and swim about in my stomach as in a glass bowl'.

After a tennis injury in which he slipped a disc, he was forced to wear a corset. He didn't relish the prospect. 'It would,' he said, 'find immediate favour in the wardrobe of a sado-masochistic transvestite.'

He spent so long making *Spartacus* that when his daughter was asked one day what he did for a living she replied, 'Spartacus.'

Acting on TV he once likened to 'being asked by the captain to entertain the passengers while the ship goes down'.

☆
☆
☆

Oliver Reed

He insists he doesn't 'put' people in hospital. But concedes, 'they sort of end up there just because I happen to be about'. The reason he gets into fights, he says, is because he's terrified of violence. 'The only thing that terrifies me more is my fear of it so I just have to go out and face it.' Other people, on the contrary, attack him because he *looks* violent. 'They think I'm a dustbin, and want to kick me over so they can see all the garbage fall out.'

He locked himself in his room for the whole day on his fortieth birthday 'being tragic' – while well-wishers sang *Happy Birthday* to him from outside the door.

He once dubbed two entire films in a day.

When a journalist asked him how he was getting on with Raquel Welch on the set of *The Four Musketeers*, he said, 'Actually I prefer her hairdresser.' (He told another writer he believed in fairies . . . with the result that the latter organized a photographer to go goblin-hunting with him.)

Comments like the following have made him the darling of every card-carrying feminist: 'I like women in their place. I like them on their knees in the kitchen, doing the dusting or whatever. In return I feed them, make them laugh, give them a punch on the nose and a good kicking when they need it . . .'

He realized from a young age that if he was ever going to achieve anything in life he would have 'to pretend to

be a sleeping volcano always with the threat of erup-
tion'.

☆
☆
☆

Before he became an actor he spent time as a hospital
porter, a taxi-driver . . . and a gigolo. In the former
capacity he proposed to about eight girls. (Another
hobby in this job was posing as a corpse and then leaping out of the coffin just as the duty nurse checked him
for rings.)

He's dyslexic, but unperturbed about it. 'If Churchill
could make it as a dunce,' he says, 'so can I.' The
teacher who tried hardest to educate him, an ex-fighter
pilot 'battling vainly against a glum group of apathetic
window-gazers', one day 'went away to a lonely place
and killed himself'.

When he dies, he wants all his friends to have a glorious wake. 'That's why I've left £10,000 out of my estate
to be spent in my local pub.'

Warren Beatty

Out of every ten stories printed about him, nine, he says, are untrue. 'If they said I was born on Pluto,' he alleges, 'people would believe it.'

Dustin Hoffman said of him, 'He's been famous longer than he's been a person.'

Midlife crisis, he says, began for him at eighteen.

He called Madonna 'more fun than a barrel of monkeys'.

Before making *Reds*, the man who ran Paramount said to him, 'Take $25 million. Go to Mexico or Peru and spend $1 million of it on a movie. Then keep the other $24 million for yourself. But don't make *Reds*.'

He thinks about his father every time he shaves because, the night before he died, he recommended a new shaving cream to him. 'He was right too,' he adds.

The most important thing you can know about women, he believes, is that they are no different from men.

He once memorized the complete works of Eugene O'Neill.

For one scene in *Bonnie & Clyde*, which he produced, he ordered a peach to be flown from another state because they were out of season in Texas, where they were shooting.

Asked once how he would characterize himself he replied, 'As someone who would not like to characterize himself.'

When Madonna was asked what he had that other men hadn't, she said, 'About a billion dollars.'

Rex Reed likened interviewing him to asking a haemophiliac for a gallon of blood. Says Beatty: 'I would rather ride down the street backwards on a camel, nude, in a snowstorm, than give what is sometimes called an in-depth interview.'

Woody Allen says that, if he's reincarnated, he wants to come back as Warren Beatty's fingertips.

Michelle Phillips, she of Mamas and Papas' fame, and a former lover, says his idea of a good time is five hours on the phone.

Joan Collins said of his libido: 'Three, four times a day, every day, wasn't usual for him. Oh, and he was able to accept phone calls at the same time.'

'He has an interesting psychology of women,' said Leslie Caron, 'he's always falling in love with girls who've just been nominated for an Academy Award.'

Mamie van Doren described him as 'a walking gland', adding, 'He's the kind of man who'll end up dying in his own arms.'

He once described monogamy as 'genius' – but that was before Annette Bening.

☆ Since becoming a dad, he has developed the following
☆ homespun theology: 'God is kind because He doesn't
☆ let you know how wonderful being a father is until it
happens to you.'

Ex-lover Britt Ekland said of him, 'He was the most
divine lover of all. His libido was as lethal as high
octane gas. He could handle women as smoothly as
operating an elevator. One flick and we were on the
way.'

Roseanne

Shortly after she was born, a restraining jacket was put over her to stop her shoving her fist into her mouth.

She did her first shoplifting at sixteen ... and was caught.

She never enjoyed playing with Barbie dolls. She wanted the doll to be a resistance fighter parachuting behind enemy lines with a secret code.

She once put a rabbit into a washing machine because its feet were dirty ... and broke its neck.

She didn't like living in her parents' house as a young child because 'it didn't smell like bread and pickles, it smelled like nail polish'.

She believes that psychiatrists have 'killed or locked away every human being who really did know how to save the world'. People in the sane world want everything dead, she says. 'Being sane is like being off-balance a little.'

She believes it's illegal to be fat in Hollywood.

The 60s didn't begin for her until 1971.

She was afraid to 'do' drugs because she felt so 'far out' *without* them.

She chews so much gum during her show that a spitoon has to be provided for her.

☆ She has an obsession with the number 5. If things don't
☆ add up to that number she believes terrible things will
☆ happen.

She has written poetry she doesn't understand, from trance-like states.

She was hit by a car when she was sixteen and believes she's been out of the world called 'Normal' since. She regards her scars from that experience as 'badges of courage gleaned from a frightening journey away from a foreign country where I never belonged'.

She likes New York because people there treat her like a person first and a celebrity second. 'Even thin people look fat there,' she says, 'and fat women are always out with handsome men, not like in California where everyone thinks fat is something you can catch, and is therefore to be avoided.'

About her sexual energy she says, 'It's just a damn shame that I'm married and there's AIDS, 'cause if there wasn't I would rip through town like a she-devil hurricane until I got tired, which would be a long, long time.' She once wrote a story about going to bed with ten men.

She regards educated people as being brain-dead, adding: 'They have that well-scrubbed look, like they reached into their brain and scrubbed it all out.'

Her ambition? 'To break every social norm, turn it back on itself and see that it's laughed at.'

Jack Nicholson

One of his first jobs in the film world consisted of sorting out the fan mail for cartoon characters Tom and Jerry.

His first marriage collapsed, he said, when his wife got into mysticism. 'I didn't want to get into a situation where I was in competition with God,' he said.

His first film, *Cry Baby Killer*, was made in ten days on a budget of $7,000.

He made twenty B movies before the breakthrough *Easy Rider* in 1969. 'Often in the morning I'd play an Indian,' he said of that period, 'then after lunch I was the soldier that killed the Indian.'

'I studied hard to play the Devil,' he said of his role in *The Witches of Eastwick* . . . 'A lot of people think I've been preparing for it all my life.'

He's been overweight since he was four, he claims. His favourite personal feature is his '1,000-watt smile' . . . because smiles can't get fat.

The President of the US doesn't know what he's going to be doing on a given day six months down the road, he says, but an actor does: 'It doesn't matter if your mother's dead or there's been an earthquake – you're still going to be out filming that movie.'

There are two ways up the ladder of success, he believes: hand over hand or clawing and scratching. 'It sure has been tough on my nails,' he adds.

☆ Considering the 'advances' in movie technology, he
☆ reckons that, if you can still portray a human being a
☆ few years from now, you'll be quite a valuable commodity.

Americans don't like sexual movies, he contends –
only sexy ones.

He feels he's been more physically dissected by movie
critics – and women – than a frog in a biology class.

If you suck a breast in a movie, he says, that's an X
cert; but if you cut one off with a sword it's PG.

'The best deterrent to marriage,' says the man who
earned the biggest pay-out of Hollywood history ($60
million for playing The Joker in *Batman*), 'is the real-
ization that you won't be able to afford the divorce.'
His view of women is straightforward: 'They hate us
and we hate them. But they're stronger and smarter,
and they don't play fair.'

He describes himself as 'the most successful actor in
the history of the movies', financially speaking. 'The
minute the studio gets the opportunity to pay me,' he
says magnanimously, '*thousands* of people make
money.' He received $7 million for *A Few Good Men*
(2 weeks' work) as opposed to $2,000 for the early cult
classic *Easy Rider*.

Before he takes a girl to bed these days, he says, 'you
have to have a medical discussion about the plague
[i.e. AIDS], so that I don't bother much'. Instead, he
says, he indulges in babytalk.

☆
☆
☆

At school he created a record by being held in detention every day for a whole school year.

For all of his youth he imagined his mother (who was only sixteen years his senior) to be his sister because his family wanted to hide his illegitimacy. He learned the truth, finally, from an article in *Time* magazine.

For years, he says, cameras have been fascinated by his teeth, but latterly it's his *eyebrows* they're fastening onto. 'It's an example of Reichian particularism,' he explains. 'People are dismembered in order to negate them. With a woman, they pick out one tit or one leg, thus simulating fetishness in the mass mind.'

☆
☆
☆

Michelle Pfeiffer

Here she is on the plight of women in films vis-à-vis sex for sale: 'Demi Moore was sold to Robert Redford for $1 million. Uma Thurman went to Mr de Niro for $40,000 – and just three years ago Richard Gere bought Julia Roberts for $3,000. I'd say that was real progress.'

She describes herself as a masochistic workaholic, saying: 'If I'm not beating myself up. I feel insecure.' She also says she's 'disgustingly serious'.

Before she became famous she used to wash fridges for her father so he could re-condition and then sell them. Her fee was fifty cents per fridge.

After doing her erotic turn on the piano in *The Fabulous Baker Boys* (and 'out-Marilyning Marilyn with her rendition of 'Making Whoopee') the piano was said to have developed *blisters*!

She was so ashamed of her appearance in her youth, she used to put on make-up before going out to collect the mail.

She grew up, she says, on a bench.

She admits she's difficult with the press: 'I try to be polite, but a lot of the time it comes across as bullshit because I'd rather not be there.'

She walked off the set of *The Russia House* until better food was found for the crew.

She's not in favour of plastic surgery at the moment, ☆
but 'when I'm an old broad maybe I'll change my mind ☆
and say "Doc, lift everything thirty feet!"' ☆

The amazing thing about human beings, she says, is
that 'when it comes to loves, no matter how beat up
you think you are, no matter how scarred or wounded
or low down you've become, you somehow muster up
the courage to open yourself up one more time.'

Before the supersonic success of the past few years she
was dreadfully insecure. 'Whenever I got a good
review I'd think the studio paid for it. I just didn't
believe that something good was being written about
me for no reason.'

She didn't become an actress so her life would be
exposed. 'In fact it's really the one thing that makes me
contemplate quitting.'

Her first acting experiences were Elvis imperson-
ations, sung into a garden hose in her backyard. 'Why
Elvis and not a girl singer I'll never know,' she says.
'Fortunately, no one ever turned the hose on me.'

She describes herself as 'overly serious', saying her
basic nature is 'dark'. 'I always believe I can handle
everything and keep all those balls in the air – and then
I can't understand why I'm crying hysterically at the
end of the day and I feel overloaded and can't sleep.'

She denies that being pretty has helped her career . . .
because every time she wants to play something like a
deserted wife, producers say to her, 'Sorry, we can't
believe anyone would ever desert *you*', and she doesn't
get the role.

Priscilla Presley

Her father, a navy lieutenant was killed in a plane crash when she was a baby. Her mother re-married and brought her up to believe the second husband was her real father. She discovered the truth when looking over some old photographs.

Her mother told her that Elvis Presley was 'a bad influence for teenage girls. He arouses things in them that shouldn't be aroused. If there's ever a mother's march against him, I'll be the first in line.'

Elvis had her balance books on her head to improve her deportment.

When she told him once that one of his songs 'lacked catchiness' he hurled a chair at her. Whenever she stated her opinions too strongly he'd remind her that men were the stronger sex. 'He liked to say that it was intended for woman to be on the left side of man, close to his heart, where she gives him strength through her support.'

He sometimes took her to visit graveyards at the dead of night to remind her how transitory everything is.

She once decided to overdose on barbiturates as a result of his neglect of her, but stopped half way through her suicide attempt.

After she became pregnant, his grandmother told her not to brush her hair over her head for fear of wrapping the umbilical cord round the baby-to-be.

She has just purchased over 50,000 items of Elvis ☆
memorabilia from Colonel Parker at a cost of $4 mil- ☆
lion. ☆

When she went to a film with Elvis they would rent out
the cinema.

She met the man she left Elvis for (Mike Stone)
through Elvis. Elvis later threatened to have him
killed; Elvis's fascination with guns became an obsession towards the end of his life. He phoned her late
one evening and said, 'Cilla, have you anyone you
want taken care of? Strictly top secret.'

During her marriage to Elvis (she later referred to it as
a 'part-time' marriage) she had to wait for him to fall
asleep first every night.

☆
☆☆
☆

Billy Connolly
★

The rooms were so small in the house he grew up in, 'you could turn the light out and be in bed before it was dark'.

He left home at the age of fourteen, but came back. Because it got dark.

He says he slept on so many floors as a struggling comedian, he can tell the difference between Axminster and Wilton by the *taste*.

The great thing about Glasgow, he feels, is that if there's a nuclear attack it'll look the same afterwards. (In addition to which, he believes you can have more fun at a Glasgow funeral than an Edinburgh wedding.)

He prefers the Bay City Rollers to Leonard Cohen.

He doesn't like boiler suits because they make you look like your bum just fainted.

He frequently wonders what a Martian would make of a football game – or how he would describe it to another Martian: 'The object is to hit the goalkeeper with the ball as often as you can. If you miss, all your pals kiss you and you feel a right eejit.'

After security men frisk him at airports, he asks them, 'Was it good for you too?'

He describes fishing as 'transcendental meditation with a punchline'.

He once flew out of Adelaide on Emu Airlines. He was ☆
5,000 feet up in the air before someone pointed out ☆
that emus can't fly. ☆

The only thing he remembers about his visit to
Germany was looking up the phone book to find out if
there were any Adolf Hitlers in it. There weren't.

Most of the cocaine-dealers in LA, he says, are mixing
the coke up with talcum powder, which has the effect
that people are 'tooting it and getting overwhelmed
with the desire to move to Florida and dye their hair
blue'.

He never ceases to be amazed at people who look into
their handkerchiefs after they blow their noses. 'What
do they expect to find – a silver sixpence?'

He gave up drinking because the hangovers made his
head feel like a telephone exchange, and his mouth
like a hedgehog's crotch.

He was married for eleven years before he found out
what a douche was.

The only thing he doesn't like about oral sex is the
view.

If he married again, he says, he'd be a bigayinamist.

When he takes off his T-shirt to sunbathe, people think
he's a milk bottle.

One of the things that mystified him about America
was 'the wee containers you got with your coffee – how
on earth do the cows get it into such a small space?'

☆
☆ He defines an intellectual as someone who can listen
☆ to the William Tell Overture without thinking of the
Lone Ranger.

The way he knows whether a politician is lying is if his lips are moving.

He was delighted when Lady Di got pregnant because 'it got me out of the news sharpish'.

There are, he says, two seasons in Scotland: June and winter.

He often worries if parrots get as sick as people.

This is how he describes a stint he spent in the Middle East: 'sand in your porridge, and every time you blow your nose it's as if the chimney had just been swept.'

He has only three words to say about Scottish Nationalism. Two of them are Scottish Nationalism – and the third is unprintable. (The true Scottish patriot, he says, misses his homeland even when he's *in* it.)

He defines a well-balanced person as someone who has a drink in both hands. (And agrees with Dean Martin that you're not really drunk if you can lie on the floor without holding on.)

On his tombstone he would like the inscription, 'God Finally Got His Attention.'

Dolly Parton

When people ask what keeps her and Carl together she says, 'Being apart'. Though, she says, if he died first she'd probably not marry again. (Carl keeps such a low profile that there was a joke going round Nashville some years ago that he didn't actually exist.)

She says of her mammaries, 'If I wasn't born with them I'd have had them made.' Another time she remarked, 'The reason my feet are so tiny is because things don't grow in the shade.' And again, 'When I try to do push-ups, they never leave the floor.'

Comparing her roles in *Nine To Five* and *The Best Little Whorehouse in Texas*, she said, 'I make a better whore than a secretary.'

The reason *Rhinestone* bombed, she believes, is because 'nobody wants to see Sylvester Stallone with his shirt on.'

When Oprah Winfrey asked her how many wigs she had, she said, 'Lemme see, there are 365 days in a year . . . ' But she only brings a mere forty with her when touring.

She lives in a twenty-three-room house with twelve walk-in closets and a reputed 3,000 sequined outfits. 'You'd never believe,' she once said to a Las Vegas audience, 'how danged expensive it is to look this cheap.'

☆ She could never be accused of a penchant for subtlety.
☆ 'When people say less is more, I say more is more. Less
☆ is less. I go for more. Why should I hide the parts of me that are extreme? I just try to make the extreme more extreme.'

Her father used to make moonshine from corn wash.

Her family was so poor, the only time she got running water was when she ran to get some.

She started writing songs when she was five, but didn't take up the guitar until a relatively late seven.

She attained her full growth (ahem) by the age of thirteen.

Sometimes she writes twenty songs a day. She's written 3,000 in all.

She sleeps with the light on, a hangover to a childhood practice of keeping a kerosene lantern burning all night to stop rats running over her bed.

When she was asked how long it took her to do her hair, she replied, 'I dunno, honey – I'm never there.'

She loves buying fitness videos and then sitting watching them while eating cookies.

Arnold Schwarzenegger

He's the world's biggest box office draw, with an income reckoned to be in the region of $30 million a year.

The US Army gave him a tank he fancied during the shooting of *Kindergarten Cop*. 'I can't wait to drive up to film premieres in it,' he said. 'Everyone will stare and I'll hand the keys to the valet, and he won't know how to drive it.'

The literal translation of his surname is 'black ploughman'.

When his father drank heavily, he used to insist Arnold wasn't his real child.

He was a timid boy growing up, with ears that stuck out over his frightened eyes. One of his father's friends called him Cinderella. At night he dreamed of becoming bigger than his father ... then he woke up crying when he found he wasn't.

From a young age he wanted to be the greatest and richest bodybuilder in the world. He once said, 'I want every single person who ever touches a weight to equate the feeling of the barbell with my name.'

He has a love interest in every one of his films – a gun.

One critic of his performance in *Conan the Barbarian*: 'He's about as emotive as a tree trunk. When he's supposed to show love for Valeria, he might as well be

☆ staring at a hunk of burlap.' (But that film grossed $9.6
☆ million in its first weekend, and took in over $100 mil-
☆ lion worldwide.)

Clive James once described him as looking like 'a condom stuffed with walnuts'.

He has £500,000-worth of cars in his garage, compris-
ing a Porsche, a Mercedes, an antique El Dorado, a
Harley Davidson motorcycle, and his latest 'toy', a
£55,000 ex-military mini-tank from the Gulf War.

He once said to a friend, 'If you told me I'd put on
muscles if I ate a kilo of shit, I'd eat it.'

Of his raunchy background he says, 'Many times while
I was getting laid, in my head I was doing a business
deal.'

'Please understand,' he tells his fans, 'that I am like
ordinary men, only bigger and stronger. Why do people treat me with fun just because I am the biggest,
strongest and most beautiful man in the world?'

Kim Basinger

★

She won a beauty contest at the age of seventeen singing 'Wouldn't It Be Luverly' from *My Fair Lady*.

In her home while growing up, she possessed ten dogs, seven cats, and sixty large inflatable ducks which she placed in the swimming pool.

Her first marriage was to a man fifteen years her senior; it lasted eight years.

Her mother thinks she's a spoiled brat, and wouldn't think twice about putting her across her knee and giving her a thorough spanking.

She described her love scenes with Mickey Rourke in *9½ Weeks*, her breakthrough movie, as like 'kissing the inside of an ashtray'.

She insists on washing her hair in Evian water.

She borrowed $500 from her father to become a New York model. Three days after she arrived in that town she was able to pay him back.

She says she earned so much money modelling overall, 'there were times I'd be walking round with as much as $25,000 in uncashed cheques in my bag, because I didn't have time to get to the bank'.

She left modelling because 'it was no fun trying to keep yourself at 115 pounds when you like ice-cream'.

☆
☆   She turned down $5 million to appear in a sequel to *9½*
☆   *Weeks*.

She puts lemon juice and sour cream in her bath water.

She loves suspender belts so much she says she even wears them *outside* her clothing.

She's allergic to sunlight, and has to hide under a parasol on bright LA days. (She has a clause in her contract freeing her from filming at high noon.) Her skin, as a result, is alabaster . . . but she dreams of one day having a tan.

She owns her own production company.

She recently recorded a rock album called *The Colour of Sex*.

She spent $20 million on a town in Georgia.

Alec Baldwin was so besotted with her on the set of *Too Hot To Handle* – which she undoubtedly was – he joined a society called Co-Dependents Anonymous to get over her. She said of her relationship with him at that time, 'There's an enormous electricity between us, but sometimes the current gets overloaded and there's a short.'

She suffered from anxiety attacks as a young girl because she felt people were undressing her with their eyes. The lasting after-effect of such sensitivity has been a persistent agoraphobia. (The doctor she attended for this condition was named Dr Ronald Doctor.)

She describes herself as being 'debilitatingly shy'. ☆
Asked how she squares this with the *outré* characters ☆
she plays on screen, she replied succinctly 'That's just ☆
acting.'

Responding to a charge that she had an off-screen fling
with Michael (*Batman*) Keaton, she said, 'The only
thing Michael and I shared away from the camera was
our mutual love of bats.'

She says she loves 'wild, crazy, wonderful, nasty sex'
. . . but also romance. (Phew!)

She wanted to take off all her clothes for a scene in
Batman until Keaton reminded her that doing so
would prevent children from seeing the finished cut.
'So I ended up eating popcorn instead,' she reflects.

She now disowns *9½ Weeks* as a glorified video . . . but
has eight hours of unscreened footage from that movie
in her home, which she watches regularly.

She won't wear jewellery because she feels her hands
are ugly.

She's not as fascinated by stardom as one might imagine,
saying, 'Sometimes I have this vision I'd just like to
walk down the street naked and leave it all behind.'

Asked why she posed nude for an eight-page
Penthouse feature, she quipped, 'I needed the exposure.'

Just in case you're wondering about her self-image, she
confesses she's no Mother Teresa, 'but I don't jump on
every man that comes into view'.

☆
☆
☆

She once vacated the set of a movie in mid-shoot to visit a psychic in Mexico.

She became an actress, she says, because 'inside me there's an anxious, terrified, out-of-your-mind need for creative expression'.

After reneging on a verbal agreement to appear in the box office flop *Boxing Helena*, the courts decreed she pay $5.3 million to the production company behind the movie. She filed a bankruptcy petition to avoid payment, but it was rejected. At her wedding to Alec Baldwin, the latter commented wryly: 'I promise to take her for better or worse, for richer or poorer . . . and to help her pay off her debts.'

A crew member irritated by her fractiousness on the set of *The Marrying Man* spoke for a lot of people when he said, 'You can have diva behaviour, but you've got to back it up with more than *hair*.'

Interviewer Jonathan van Meter called her 'the most self-indulgent, dumb, irritating person I've ever met'.

Sean Connery

He dropped out of school at thirteen to drive a milk wagon.

He regards talking to journalists as a practice akin to 'screwing in public'.

Ursula Andress says of his 'beatnik casualness': 'Even if you *did* persuade him to wear a suit for a business meeting, you'd probably discover he had no socks on.'

When he was judged to be the Sexiest Man Alive in a poll a few years back, he quipped, 'Are there sexy dead ones?'

He doesn't believe there's anything 'particularly' wrong with hitting a woman 'although I don't recommend doing it in the same way that you'd hit a man. An open-handed slap is justified if all other alternatives fail.' Which is rather understanding of him, when you think of it . . .

Says long-time friend Terence Young: 'He could live without films, but I doubt he could survive without golf.'

Every time he starts a movie, he claims, he gets lip-sores from nervousness.

He said of the prohibitive taxes introduced by Chancellor Denis Healey in the mid-70s: 'I was one of the most successful actors around, and yet I didn't have a pot to piss in.' (He was paying up to 98% tax on some of his earnings at that time.)

☆
☆
☆

His movie *Robin and Marian* was originally intended to be called *The Death of Robin Hood*, but was changed, he asserts, 'because Americans don't like persons who die'.

Like most Celts, he admits he's moody. He walked off the set of *Goldfinger* because a lady interviewing him thought that Gert Frobe – the eponymous character – was female.

Films are beautiful, he says, especially well-organized ones. 'Because in life, *nothing* works.'

To get anywhere in life, he believes, you have to be anti-social; otherwise you'll get devoured. 'So I don't go around with a Welcome mat round my neck.'

You can make your own mind up as to whether he suffers from (enjoys?) the legendary Scottish tight-fistedness from the following quote: 'I want all the money I can get. I'm entitled to it. I don't believe all this stuff about starving in a garret, or being satisfied with artistic appreciation only.'

He's only twelve years older than Harrison Ford – yet played his father in *Indiana Jones And The Last Crusade*.

His pay cheque for a forty-five second cameo as Richard the Lionheart in *Robin Hood: Prince of Thieves* was a cool $500,000.

He underwent a health scare in 1992 when three white spots were discovered on his larynx, but laser surgery removed them successfully. Afterwards his wife joked about the temporary loss of his voice: 'He couldn't swear as much as he would have liked to on the golf course.'

He can't contemplate ever retiring.

☆
☆
☆

Elizabeth Taylor

★

In *The New Yorker* in 1975, Pauline Kael wrote, 'The highpoint in her acting career came when she was twelve.' (That was the year she made *National Velvet*). Three years later she contemplated 'retiring'.

In *Giant* she played a character that aged from eighteen to fifty.

Mike Todd once said of their relationship: 'We had more fun fighting than most couples do making love.' Richard Burton might have agreed some years later.

She was converted to Judaism in 1959, and was rechristened Elisheba Rachel.

According to one writer, she was so much the property of MGM that 'nothing except illness happened to her by accident'.

Her troubles all started, she said, because she has the body of a woman and the mind of a child.

She says she has a lust for diamonds that's almost like a disease.

When people run up to her these days, she claims, it's not to ask for her autograph so much as to get a closer look at her *wrinkles*.

After going to bed with her for the first time, Richard Burton is alleged to have commented. 'I am worth $4 million more than I was yesterday.' It was probably true, whether that was his motivation or not. By the late 60s they were the top-earning husband-and-wife team in any business in the world, apart from the British and Dutch monarchies.

Her life has been a saga of ill-health. Her first time in a cast was 1954. A year later she was on crutches from sciatica. Some time later a steel splinter was flung in her eye by a wind machine. She was bedridden for two months after having her first child. It's said she had a minor heart attack in 1953, and she nearly died in 1992 from flu complications. In 1959 she claims to have stopped breathing four times when she contracted a rare form of pneumonia and was given an hour to live.

She's noted for her contributions to charity. According to Richard Burton, 'She supported the entire Biafran War effort on her own'.

Richard Burton once gave her a diamond that Shah Jahan had given his wife in 1621 ... with the Taj Mahal. 'I set out to buy that too,' he said, 'but it was a little difficult to transport to Switzerland.'

Gerard Depardieu

The literal translation of his surname means: 'Oh my God.'

He had a lucky youth, he says, 'because my father was dead drunk all day'.

He describes his mother as being constantly pregnant, babies popping out of her stomach 'at an industrial rate, like real little ping pong balls'.

In his first job (apprentice in a print shop) he was earning £7 a month.

He became a Muslim between the ages of fifteen and seventeen.

He once 'half scared a woman to death' on a train. 'I was dirty,' he remembers, 'and she looked down her nose at me. So I pulled a face, gave myself a tic and grinned horribly . . . it was my earliest little piece of cinema.'

If he hadn't been an actor, he claims he would have been a killer, adding, 'If you're playing a murderer, you never stop killing people in your head.'

He made seventy-eight films from 1971–91, going nude in thirteen of them. He considers his body as 'just an envelope of flesh around me'.

He worked with Robert de Niro in Bertolucci's *1990*. One scene called de Niro to cry, but the tears wouldn't come. Then suddenly he hit Depardieu and snapped his fingers for the camera to roll. 'I'm sorry, Gerard,' he said afterwards, 'but I need to hurt somebody I love in order to cry.' Depardieu replied, 'Listen, my boy, I don't want to shoot this scene fifty times if that's what it's going to take to make you cry.'

Asked if he was bisexual, he said, 'Look, we're all animals. I prefer *les filles* at the moment, but who knows, maybe in a few years . . . *bof*!'

Catherine Deneuve, he once said, 'is the man I've always wanted to be'.

A crew member said working with him was confusing because he always hits the marks when 'Action!' is called, but afterwards 'he goes off into the middle of the desert and gets blotto on a huge forty-eight-hour bender'. A critic said, 'He can go, in a split second, from slipping a frog down the dress of a script girl to throwing himself at the bedside of his dying mother.'

He hates mirrors because there are very few moments when he actually feels good about himself.

He doesn't want to become a Schwarzenegger or make special-effect films. 'I *am* a special effect,' he says modestly.

He describes acting as 'escaping into reality'.

Hamlet bores him to tears.

His children, he says, 'sometimes look at me like I'm a crazy man'. With some reason, one would have imagined . . .

Here's his overall self-summation: 'I will always be an actor who smokes French cigarettes, eats like crazy, drinks too much wine, rides a motorbike . . . and doesn't give a damn what he looks like.'

☆
☆
☆

Sharon Stone

She's so hot at the moment that the producers don't feel they even need Michael Douglas to sell *Basic Instinct 2*. She earned $3 million for her role in *Intersection* opposite Richard Gere. 'They'd pay me to play Lassie,' she says. As against that, $50 million was invested in *Sliver* and only $35 million was recouped.

She refused to appear with Clint Eastwood in the smash hit *In the Line of Fire* because he wasn't a big enough star any more.

She believes all men are dogs – and sooner or later they start to bark. The most interesting parts of her dates these days, she claims, are when she retreats to the ladies' room with a good book under her arm.

'If you have a vagina and a point of view in Hollywood,' she says, 'that's a lethal combination.' Adding humbly, 'If I was just normally intelligent I could probably get away with it – but I'm *fiercely* intelligent – and that's threatening.'

The most beneficial side-effect of fame, she believes, is that it has enabled her to 'torture a higher class of man' than was her privilege heretofore.

Her penchant for divesting herself of her underwear underwhelmed her *Sliver* co-star, Willy Baldwin. When she removes same in a central scene from that movie, he remarked off-camera to her: 'Me and the rest of the world have already seen it: it's no big deal.'

She posed nude in *Playboy* some years ago simply ☆
because 'I wanted to get noticed' ... and the rest is ☆
herstory. 'I would like to have been accepted on the ☆
integrity of my work,' she said afterwards, 'but after
years in the business it became a decision as to
whether I was prepared to take my clothes off in order
to work. And I was.'

She doesn't regard herself as glamorous, 'but I can *do*
glamour. I can make it happen, turn the dial up or
down – but it's not real.'

Here's her view on image: 'The funny thing about cre-
ating one is that people seem to buy into it as the reality. Then you start to *act* like that's how you are. Then
you become it!'

Bill McDonald, the executive producer of *Sliver*, left
his newly-wed wife for her during the making of that
movie – and McDonald's own wife, in turn, started
dating Joe Eszterhas.

She says she's got a love-hate relationship with director Paul Verhoeven: 'He loves me and I hate him.'

The controversial scene in *Basic Instinct*, where she
crosses her legs *sans* underwear caused one wag to
remark: 'Sharon's gynaecologist can now make a diag-
nosis by going to the multiplex and sitting down front.'

Woody Allen

His idea of a holiday is to lie in his bed in his New York apartment with the blinds drawn and the air-conditioning on full blast.

He has a problem with interviewers. 'They keep asking me if there's going to be an Armageddon,' he explains, 'and, if so, will it be before or after tea.'

'All of the films I've done,' he says, 'are personal failures. None of them leave me with a good feeling. When I've finished them I don't want to see them again.' He claims to be awaiting the day he'll be 'found out'.

He once said of his first wife: 'She was a philosophy student and we had these long discussions in which she always proved I didn't exist.'

'Life you can't control,' he says, 'only art. Art and masturbation.'

He eats out 365 days a year.

He gets nervous crossing the road 'in case some guy in a car decides to make himself famous and lets his foot slip off the brake onto the accelerator as I pass'.

His father was an engraver of jewellery.

'My teachers all loathed me,' he says of his schooldays. 'My parents were called to the schools so often my friends still recognize them on the street.'

He says his father still thinks his films are 'crap', and
would have much preferred it if he went on to become
a pharmacist 'and made $125 a week for the rest of my
life, with a pension'.

He started his creative career writing gags for a
Manhattan agent for $25 a week.

When he became a stand-up comic he was hardly earning his cab fare to the venue, says a source. He once
stopped his act to tell an audience they were the worst
he had ever played to and deserved a place in *The
Guinness Book of Records*. But they were too busy
chatting to hear his gripe.

Colleague Jack Rollins describes him as 'the shyest
man I've ever met'. When he was nineteen he won an
award but was too embarrassed to collect it, so went
home instead.

In general he feels life is divided into the horrible and
the miserable.

His first wife he remembers as being immature: 'I'd be
in the bath and she'd come in and sink my boats.'

He sees life as being divided between the good and
bad people: the good ones sleep better, but the bad
ones enjoy the waking hours more.

He's not the fittest guy in the world: in fact he was once
overtaken by two people pushing a car.

He believes sex is only dirty if you're doing it right.

He defines his brain as his second favourite organ.

☆
☆
☆

'Sex is a beautiful thing between two people,' he says, 'but between five it's *fantastic.*'

He spent years in analysis, he says, because he was breastfed on falsies.

Marriage, he claims, 'is just something that happens to you. Like blight.'

Life he defines succinctly as a 'concentration camp'.

He doesn't watch funny movies; he watches Ingmar Bergman.

He once failed to make a chess team, he says, because of his height.

He says he suffers from 'anhedonia', which is an inability to enjoy pleasure, and also 'entering phobia'. He fantasizes about vanishing into a disembodied presence, free to roam at will without interference or the need to communicate.

He's been nominated for fourteen Oscars in the last twelve years. He refused to collect the three he won (two for *Annie Hall* and one for *Hannah and Her Sisters*). His excuse on the first occasion was that it clashed with his clarinet gig at Michael's bar.

Gene Wilder said he makes movies 'as if he were lighting 10,000 safety matches to illuminate a city'.

The problem with his first wife, he said, was that he kept putting her under a pedestal.

He likes to visit his mother on Mother's Day because 'it's like taking a refresher course in guilt'.

He said of *Manhattan*: 'If it makes one more person miserable, I feel I'll have done my job.'

It would be a huge relief to him, he claims, if someone said to him, 'You cannot make another film.'

Generally he feels you've got to hate yourself to have any integrity at all.

Sex without love is an empty experience for him, 'but, as empty experiences go, it's one of the best'.

More than any other time in history, he feels, man faces a crossroads. 'One path leads to despair and utter hopelessness; the other to total extinction. Let us pray we have the wisdom to choose correctly.'

Love is the answer to life, he believes, 'but while you're waiting for the answer, sex raises some pretty good questions'.

Not only does he not believe in God, 'but try getting a plumber at the weekend'.

He doesn't want to become immortal through his work, he says – but by not dying.

Sex between two people is beautiful, he says – if you can get between the right two people.

He's not afraid of dying – he just doesn't want to be there when it happens.

He's not sure about the hereafter, but he's still bringing a change of underwear.

His one regret in life is that he's not somebody else.

Melanie Griffith

She's lived life in the fast lane from a young age. When she was fourteen, she says, half of her friends had had abortions. At fifteen she was hooked on booze and drugs, and for the next thirteen years ravaged her body with a heavy cocktail of cocaine, alcohol and forty cigarettes a day.

Her love life is nothing if not unusual. She met *Miami Vice* star Don Johnson when she was fourteen (he was eighteen years older than her), lived with him at sixteen, married him at eighteen, divorced after four months, then married Stephen Bauer, then divorced him . . . and re-married Johnson in 1989. That marriage lasted until March 1993, whereupon she filed for divorce again.

She's always been accident-prone. As a teenager she was mauled by one of the lions her mother kept at home. At twenty-two, when drunk, she was nearly killed by a car on Sunset Boulevard.

She has a pear tattoo on her left buttock!

She loves being blonde because 'men automatically think you're dumb and that they can say anything. They fall into the trap every time, revealing amazing things about themselves.'

Hitchcock once gave her a present of a tiny coffin with a little dead mother inside.

Elvis Presley

His twin brother Jesse died at birth, a fact which gave him a lifelong feeling that he was only half a person – and that he had to do twice as much to justify his existence.

His mother bought him his first guitar. He really wanted a bicycle, but they couldn't afford one.

Whenever he went to the movies with his daughter Lisa-Marie, he used to rent out the entire theatre to avoid being besieged by fans.

He had a habit of watching up to three televisions simultaneously, in order to hear all the different news broadcasts at one time.

His least favourite TV personality was Robert Goulet. One time when the latter was on screen, he shot his set to pieces.

'I know nothing about music,' he said once. 'In my line of business you don't have to.'

There's a groundswell of opinion that he committed suicide – or was even murdered – on 16 August 1977.

According to his bodyguards, he used to burn down buildings in his grounds because he 'felt like it'. On another occasion, he's reputed to have chartered a jet to travel 1,000 miles to procure a particular type of junk food he fancied.

☆ The youngest official Elvis impersonator is three and
☆ the oldest seventy-eight. In all, his lookalikes can be
☆ found in seventy-eight different countries. Wales's
Peter Singh, who wears a turban and beard, claims to
be the only Sikh Elvis impressionist.

Financially, he's more successful now than when he
was alive.

He was eighteen stone when he died. Pirated copies of
his post-mortem are alleged to have sold for up to
$5,000 a go.

A British bookmaker is offering odds of 1,000/1 on the
following treble: that Martians will land on earth, the
Loch Ness monster will be discovered, and that Elvis
will be found alive somewhere.

The last part of that treble might be worth a flutter, as
a recent public sighting of The King had him piling
groceries into takeaway bags at a supermarket in
Santa Barbara. He has also recently re-married, by all
reports, but isn't really happy with his latest wife and is
considering applying for a sex change before fleeing to
Peru, where he plans to join an enclosed Order of
transvestite orang-utans for Group Therapy.

Sam Shepard

His name is Sam Shepard Rogers. In keeping with the family tradition, he was nicknamed Steve to distinguish him from his father, who was also Sam Rogers. 'My name came down from seven generations of men with the same name,' he says, 'each naming the first son the same as the father, then the mothers nicknaming the sons so as not to confuse them with the fathers when hearing their names called in the open air while working side-by-side in the waist-high wheat.'

He hasn't much nostalgia for his youth, saying, 'The fifties sucked dogs, man.'

When he writes, he says, 'I get the haunting feeling that something in me writes but it's not necessarily me.'

When he started writing, he says there was a feeling abroad 'that in order to be a true artist you had to do yourself in or go bananas, so that your insanity became a badge of honour. I knew guys who walked off roofs.'

He remains underwhelmed about the trappings of Hollywood fame: 'It's all about vanity. Everything is attended to. Would you like some Perrier? Anything we can do? May we throw ourselves on the ground in front of you? This unbelievable barrage of indulgence.' (He once defined collaboration with a producer as 'Don't forget to kiss ass from beginning to end.')

When he goes to films, he says, 'I am the screen, I'm not me. I look at my life afterwards and I hate it not being a movie. I hate having to eat, having to work, having to sleep, having to go to the bathroom, having to live in this body which isn't a star's body and all the time knowing stars exist.'

Richard Harris

When he was involved in pub brawls, he says he was called Irish, but when he won acting plaudits he was automatically British.

He's the middle son of a large family, 'which means you're inclined to get lost amid the noise of all the others – so you make your own noise'.

When he married Anna Turkel, the magistrate asked, 'Do you take this woman to be your lawful wedded wife?' . . . and before he could say anything, she piped up 'He does!'

He believes sex ruins marriage.

Critic Tony Crawley called him the 'singularly best media manipulator' he knows, adding, 'If a distant relation broke wind he could make a story out of it.'

He doubts he could ever write his autobiography, 'because I was far too drunk to ever recall what happened'.

One of his favourite epigrams is 'The world owes no one anything – and all we owe *it* is a death'.

In a scene in *Mutiny on the Bounty*, Brando had to hit him, but he did so too gently according to Harris. After a few re-takes with similar results he said to The Mumbling One: 'Shall we dance?' After that incident, Brando played any scene he had with Harris to a stand-in. Harris, for his part procured a little green box, drew Brando's features on it, and played to that. The two men didn't speak to one another for close to a quarter century afterwards.

Neither did he get on famously with Sam Peckinpah, who directed him in *Major Dundee*. Peckinpah subsequently said he preferred the snakes in that film to the actors.

James Booth called him a narcissist. Rod Taylor saw him as an angel. For Kevin Barker he was a bigot – and for John Philip Law a baby.

The most distinctive characteristic of a successful politician, he feels, is 'selective cowardice'.

Steven Spielberg

He was regarded as a wimp at school. His nickname was The Retard.

He says he grew up in a house with 'three screaming younger sisters and a mother who played concert piano with seven others'.

He swallowed a transistor at the age of fifteen.

He used to vomit in the science lab when asked to dissect frogs.

'If I hadn't been a boy scout,' he once said, rather mysteriously, 'I would probably have ended up as an axe murderer or a butcher in a Jewish deli.'

Critic Tony Crawley said of *1941*, the first film of his mature career to bomb at the box office, 'He almost *needed* a flop to make him appear human.'

'I always think of the audience when I'm directing,' he says, ' . . . because I *am* the audience.' (In 1985 he said, 'When I grow up, I still want to be a director.')

He made his first full-scripted film at thirteen.

Of the reliability of UFO spottings he says, 'Men have been executed for murder on less evidence.'

Frank Marshall, his sometime producing partner, says he gets a new idea approximately every thirteen seconds.

He described the movie *ET* as 'my last summer vacation before going back to school'. Of ET the *character*
he said, 'It took seventeen human hearts to make *his*
heart beat once . . . and he was STILL cheaper than
Marlon Brando!'

He once made a film about what happens to rain when
it hits dirt.

The most expensive habit in the world, he feels, isn't
heroin – but celluloid. And he needs a fix approximately once every two years.

Burt Reynolds

His father was a police chief ... who once put him behind bars.

Asked to describe his observations of Lee Strasburg's Actor's Studio, he said succinctly: 'Seventeen Marlon Brandos and thirteen James Deans.'

He was sacked from Universal Studios on the same day as Clint Eastwood. Eastwood was informed his Adam's apple stuck out too far, while Reynolds was simply told he had no talent. 'I may learn to act some day,' he joked to Eastwood afterwards, 'but you'll never get rid of that Adam's apple.'

Asked once what his idea of the perfect woman was, he replied, 'A unique combination of courtesan and lady.'

At the peak of his womanizing, he told *Playboy*, he had trouble remembering the names of the women he went to bed with – or, indeed, how he got there.

By the end of 1968 he had five movies in the can but none released. He dubbed himself, 'The most popular unknown in Hollywood.'

He did an all-but-nude centrefold for *Playboy* in 1972.

Hollywood is okay, but he'd generally prefer to be 'on a farm with a few cases of beer'.

Unfazed by the negative reviews of middlebrow critics that have plagued him throughout his topsy-turvy career, he says of himself: 'I look at the camera as someone I've been having an affair with for the past twenty years – and who's only just realized how good in bed I am.'

'I became the World's Number One box-office star,' he said once, 'not because of my movies but in spite of 'em.'

He believes that 'if a woman thinks she's sexy, she *is*'.

At his peak he said, 'Nobody is worth what they pay me.'

He once said he could sing as well as Fred Astaire could act.

The first time he attempted to direct a movie, he asked Mel Brooks for advice on how to look impressive. 'Fire someone the first day,' said Brooks.

The secret behind the success of *Smokey and the Bandit* and *Cannonball Run*, he claims, was the fact that audiences were laughing so much, they couldn't hear the lines. 'If they did, they'd have thrown up,' he adds.

He told *Playboy* magazine in 1979, 'Being boring is a bigger sin than killing and maiming.'

He would like to direct a movie, he says, because it's getting too hard to hold his stomach in any more.

He enjoyed the recent *Twin Peaks* series, because 'it gave me a chance to see a lot of actors I thought were dead'.

Jackie Collins

She married Wallace Austin, a wealthy Londoner, in 1960. 'I think I married him,' she said later, 'because everybody said I couldn't.' Four years later, Austin was found dead in a car in Hampshire. 'He was a manic depressive,' she says. She believes he overdosed on his medication.

She can't type.

When asked if the Tinseltown sexploits that line her books are based on fact she replied, 'Yes, but I toned them down.'

If she hears something spicy at a Hollywood party she tends to go into a toilet and write it down in case she forgets it.

The typical Hollywood wife, according to her, 'gets up in the morning, has her session with her exercise coach, has a massage, has her nails fixed. Then she eats a lettuce leaf at Ma Maison, where she pays a fortune for it. She bitches to her lady friends that her husband is no longer sleeping with her, but someone else. Then she and her friends set off for La Grande shop where they will buy things they don't need, like a $3,000 fun fur. Then she goes home, yells at a Mexican maid, and says to her husband when he comes home from the studio exhausted, "Let's have a party tonight".'

She has traditionally been irked at being seen as 'Joan Collins's little sister' and once toyed with the idea of changing her name. The reason she didn't was because

☆
☆
☆

she felt she would then be seen as 'Joan-Collins's-Little-Sister-Who-Changed-Her-Name'.

She expects to live to eighty-five. At that age she intends to invite all her relatives in, videotape them, secretly study the tapes, and figure out which ones want the money. 'Then I'll give it to the one who doesn't want anything.'

Further, she intends to leave the real names of her novel characters in a little black box to be opened after her death.

Gabriel Byrne

When he informed his parents he was going to be an actor, they were unimpressed. 'I might as well have told them I was going into space,' he muses.

Before becoming an actor he spent time as a bartender, a maid(!), a plumber and a journalist – and he has written a novel. Plumbing was the least memorable of all. 'They kept sending me on errands hoping I'd get lost,' he remembers.

He also spent four years studying to be a priest. This was the period of his life where he became addicted to drinking altar wine ... and eating congealed candle grease!

His first girlfriend, he says, was 'a frail, dark-haired convent girl who loved Fabian, Billy Fury, Sal Mineo and me – in that order'.

He once brought fifty-seven girls to Spain on a would-be cultural excursion when he was a Spanish teacher, 'but only succeeded in igniting the fire of fifty-seven love affairs'. 'There were guys everywhere, hanging over the balconies. At the end of every evening we had to prise people apart with crowbars.'

His son, he says, has travelled more in his three years than Byrne's own father did in an entire lifetime.

Jack Lemmon

★

An only child, he was born prematurely, with acute jaundice. 'Just wanted to get a little extra attention,' he claims . . . 'Actors are impossible, you know.'

He had three mastoid and seven adenoid operations by the time he was thirteen. According to his mother, 'he popped in and out of hospitals like a cork on the Great Salt Lakes'.

He hated his surname so much he once tinkered around with the idea of changing it to 'Lemon', but didn't because he feared he might be mistaken for Lenin.

His father, a flour-mixer, once told him he didn't care what he did with his life so long as he did it passionately. 'The day I don't find romance in a loaf of bread,' he commented enigmatically, 'I'll quit.'

He wasn't a very good Harvard student, on his own admission: 'The only reason I know French is because I flunked the course so many times it sunk in by osmosis.'

His first accommodation in New York, having abandoned the idea of an academic life in favour of acting, was, as he puts it, 'a windowless linen closet'.

He said of *Airport 77*, one of his few turkeys on celluloid, 'It should have sunk along with the airplane.'

He began to be worried about his career when an emergency meeting was called during the shooting of the movie *Pffft* to decide whether there should be three Fs in the title or just two.

If he had to sit through any of his own movies twice, he insists, he'd go mad: 'I tend to munch on popcorn, saying, 'No, no, you fool, you're lousing up the picture.'

He insists he finds it impossible to be funny in real life, even if his life depended on it.

Frank Sinatra

His career was so low in 1953 he said he'd *pay* Harry Cohn to let him have the role of Maggio in *From Here To Eternity*. Ava Gardner said, 'He'll kill himself if he doesn't get it.' Sinatra himself said, 'I know Maggio. I went to school with him in Hoboken. I was beaten up with him. I might have *been* Maggio.'

He was so elated when he won the Oscar for that role he went for a walk with the statuette ... and was accused of stealing it by a Beverly Hills policeman.

'If it hadn't been for my interest in music,' he said once, 'I'm convinced I would have ended up in crime.' Rival Bing Crosby said, 'He's always nurtured a secret desire to be a hood but he's got too much class to go that route so he gets his kicks out of barking at newsmen instead.'

His problems with the media are well-documented. He once described journalists as a breed of being who 'lie in the sun all day and then go home and lie some more'. (That was before Kitty Kelley). He spoke collectively of the media as 'bums, parasites, hookers and pimps'.

Said John Huston of him, 'He thinks heaven is a place where there are all broads and no newspapermen. He doesn't know he'd be better off if it were the other way round.' Marlon Brando, who quarrelled with him on the set of *Guys and Dolls*, said: 'He's the kind of guy who, when he dies, he gonna give God a hard time for making him bald.'

☆
☆
☆

The mother of Mia Farrow, his third wife, is only four years older than him.

The stories of his female conquests are legendary but he doesn't totally corroborate them. 'If they were all true,' he said once, 'I would now be speaking to you from a jar in Princeton.'

On a scale of one to ten, he rates his voice as a poor six.

He recently offered $5,000 to anyone who could identify the hit-and-run driver who killed his pet dog.

David Lynch

His early childhood was too happy. 'I kept waiting for something weird to happen,' he says.

His mother refused to give him colouring books. Instead she gave him blank sheets of paper. Here his love of painting blossomed.

His favourite toy was a knife.

He was fired from most of his early jobs. They included binman, animal dissector and deliverer of *The Wall Street Journal*.

His first film concerned a distraught bed-wetting boy, abused by his parents, who secretly grows a benevolent grandmother from a seed.

He thinks of *Blue Velvet* as a love story.

He has a habit of wearing one shoelace untied.

His friend Mel Brooks described him as 'Jimmy Stewart from Mars'. Says Lynch, 'I'm sure he meant it as a compliment'.

He once said he wished he could be in the world of *Twin Peaks* all the time.

He apologizes to his die-hard fans for the fact the *Wild At Heart* had a happy ending.

In his house he has a bottle containing a friend's uterus. The surgeon performing the hysterectomy saved the tissue for him on the patient's request.

☆ He meditates daily in two separate 'sessions'.
☆
☆ For seven years he ordered the same meal at the Big Boy Diner . . . at 2.30pm every afternoon.

One of his paintings is called 'When I Returned, There Were Bugs in My House and Blood in the Streets'.

He writes a weekly comic strip cartoon for the *LA Reader* called 'The Angriest Dog in the World'. It concerns a canine so outraged about things that it cannot move. The images remain static from week to week; only the captions change.

He lists his off-screen hobbies as 'dental hygiene and spark plugs'.

Alec Guinness

He had three different names until the age of fourteen, and lived in about thirty different hotels, lodgings and flats during that time.

His brother was stricken with polio at the age of eleven. 'Let him recover,' he said to God, 'and I will never put an obstacle in his way should he ever wish to become a Catholic.'

He played eight different parts in *Kind Hearts & Coronets*.

When he told his fiancée's mother of his engagement to her daughter, she said, 'And the cook's just given notice!' . . . and then promptly fainted.

In 1955, James Dean showed him his new car, saying, 'She'll do 150.' 'Please never get in it,' Alec said. 'If you get in that car you'll be found dead in it by this time next week.' At 4pm the following Friday, his words came true.

His favourite performer is Ronnie Barker.

He recently declined an 'admirable' script when he found that the character he was asked to play was required to 'scramble up the side of some giant jungle waterfall clinging to overhanging ferns'. At seventy-plus years, it wasn't exactly what the doctor ordered, he felt.

☆
☆
☆
So many of his friends have died in the past forty years, he says, his address book 'begins to look like an old English country churchyard, with RIP engraved on lichen-covered stones'.

Here's his description of the Bible: 'An unreliable history of a Bronze Age tribe who had an unhealthy passion for collecting the foreskins of Philistines.'

And this is what he feels about the 'new' Catholic Mass: 'The banality and vulgarity of the translations which have ousted the sonorous Latin and Greek are of a supermarket quality which is quite unacceptable. Hand-shaking and embarrassed smiles or smirks have replaced the older courtesies: kneeling is out, queueing is in, and the general tone is rather like a BBC radio broadcast for tiny tots.'

Anthony Quinn

When he was three, his father told him he had been found in a pigsty and adopted.

He originally wanted to be a preacher, and then an architect.

When he was given a questionnaire from school to fill in, his father wrote after Nationality: 'Turkish, Italian, Chinese, Hindustan, Japanese, Mongolian, Mexican, Irish, Aztec and Scandinavian.'

He made his first pass at a girl at the age of six. 'Learn to handle them,' his grandfather advised him solemnly, 'and you'll be able to handle anything from wildcats to higher mathematics.'

His first job was shoe-shining in front of the church. Sometimes he shone the socks as well.

He didn't learn to read until he was nine.

When he was walking down the street one day he saw his sister being abducted by a man. He picked up an axe and struck him repeatedly. When he got home his father whipped him, saying, 'The first time you hit the man was for what he was doing to your sister. That was right. The second time you hit him in anger, and that might have been all right too, but the third and fourth time was because you're a potential murderer, so I'm going to whip you so that you'll never lose your temper to the point where you can kill a man.'

☆
☆
☆

His grandmother, who had cancer, said she wouldn't die until he made it in the movies. When he brought his first favourable review home to her she said, 'Now I can die in peace.' She died two weeks later.

He once dated a mother and daughter. The former was eighteen years older than him but he still wanted to marry her.

He secured his first part (in *The Plainsman*) by pretending he was a Cheyenne Indian who couldn't speak English.

He has a recurring dream about the world coming to an end. One time he nearly strangled his wife when he was waking up from a nightmare, imagining her to be a panther about to devour him.

His greatest fear, he once said, was anonymity. He would have killed to avoid it.

He used to run half a mile backwards every morning during his boxing days.

He once said he wanted to be Napoleon, Michelangelo, Shakespeare, Picasso, Martin Luther and Jack Dempsey all rolled into one.

Mickey Rooney

He went from being the world number one box-office star at the age of eighteen, to playing bit parts in beach movies at forty-eight.

He once took an overdose of sleeping pills when suffering from depression and was out cold for fourteen hours.

He made his stage debut at the age of two. He received a special Oscar for 'contribution' at the age of eighteen.

His life has been so riotous and action-packed that when one producer was offered it to film, he refused, saying: 'Who would believe it?'

When he was fifty-eight he made a rather elliptical pronouncement: 'I'm in pretty good shape for the shape I'm in.'

Regarding his typecasting, he said: 'I was a fourteen-year-old-boy for thirty years of my life'.

He was so nervous on his wedding night with Ava Gardner – his first wife – that he put on his pyjama top backwards.

He's been married so many times – eight in all – he says he's the only man whose marriage licence has 'To Whom it May Concern' on it. And when he says 'I do', the judge replies, 'I know, I know.'

☆ He's got a somewhat schizoid attitude to his life and
☆ times. 'Had I been brighter,' he said some years ago in
☆ elegiac mood, 'had the ladies been gentler, the scotch
weaker, the gods kinder, the dice hotter . . . it might all
have ended up in a one-sentence story.'

Julia Roberts

Many of her films have had her in rather dire predicaments. In *Steel Magnolias* she played a young mother dying of a diabetic condition. *Flatliners* had her as a quack experimental doctor. In *Sleeping With the Enemy* she was the terrified victim of a psychotic wife-beater . . . and in *Dying Young* she played the lover of a man stricken with terminal cancer.

On the set of one of her films, which called for her to remove certain items of her clothing, she requested the technicians and camermen to follow suit – or even trousers. The shyest one of all, she was amused to learn, had the most off-the-wall underwear.

Here's why she says she likes acting: 'I've been a pizza waitress, I've been a prostitute, I've died and come back. Who else can say that at twenty-five?'

She decided to marry Lyle Lovett just three days before the nuptials. This was just as impetuous as her decision *not* to marry Kiefer Sutherland just twenty-four hours before the ceremony was due to take place.

Asked to describe herself, she said: 'Several personalities live within me – an experienced woman, an adolescent and an innocent girl. These multiple personalities have allowed me to cope with the pressures of fame. I'm also full of contradictions. I go jogging every morning and work out in the gym, then at dinner I drink five cups of coffee.'

The writer of *Steel Magnolias*, which netted her an Oscar nomination (as did *Pretty Woman*), said of that weepie: 'There were enough tears shed on that movie to reverse the drought in Kansas.'

☆
☆
☆

Robert Redford

His parents are second-generation Irish Americans with Scottish connections.

His father, an accountant by trade, became a milkman to supplement his earnings.

When he was nineteen he became a pavement artist in Paris.

He once walked down Broadway in his pajamas in broad daylight and sat for an hour in a trash can in 57th Street 'just to see what would happen'. (The answer was . . . nothing much.)

He proposed to his wife from a pay-phone in New York.

His first child was a cot death victim at two months.

During the making of *The Hot Rock* he scaled a twenty-foot prison wall and dropped out of a hovering helicopter onto the roof of an abandoned house.

He once drove a ski-car over a cliff. Another time the accelerator of his Porsche got stuck at floorboard level as he gunned down a mountain road.

He believes he could have reached Wimbledon standard if he concentrated more on his tennis.

He refers to Hollywood as 'that tiny, ugly little street'.

☆ *Robert de Niro* ☆

He learned the entire Latin
Mass by heart before playing a
priest in *True Confessions*

☆ *Peter O'Toole* ☆

He insists he was brought up as
a girl for the first twelve years
of his life

☆ *Oliver Reed* ☆

When he dies he wants all his friends to have a glorious wake. 'That's
why I've left £10,000 out of my estate to be spent in my local pub'

☆ *Mickey Rooney* ☆

Regarding his typecasting, he said:
'I was a fourteen-year-old for thirty years of my life'

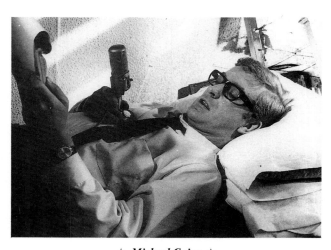

☆ *Michael Caine* ☆

When he was young he was called Old Snake Eyes,
because he never blinked

☆ *Alec Guinness* ☆

When he told his fiancée's mother of his engagement to her
daughter, she said: 'And the cook's just given notice!' . . .
and then prompty fainted

☆ *Anthony Quinn* ☆

When he was three, his father told him he had been found in a
pigsty and adopted

☆ *Elizabeth Taylor* ☆

She's noted for her contributions to charity. According to Richard
Burton, she supported the entire Biafran War effort on her own

☆ *Kim Basinger* ☆

She borrowed $500 from her father to become a New York model;
in three days she was able to pay him back

☆ *Sigourney Weaver* ☆

Sigourney's real name is Susan. She changed it to Sigourney from a character in *The Great Gatsby*, because it was 'long and curvy'

☆ *Goldie Hawn* ☆

She once drove a complete stranger, who was in labour, to a hospital and stayed by her bedside for two hours

☆ *Marilyn Monroe* ☆
Asked what she wore on her wedding night, she said: 'Chanel No 5'

☆ *Marlene Dietrich* ☆
Asked once if she would ever retire, she replied:
'That depends on the applause'

☆ ***Errol Flynn*** ☆
He was a spy for the Nazis during the Second World War

☆ *Dustin Hoffman* ☆

'A lustful nerd' is how he described himself at high school

☆ *Mel Gibson* ☆

Asked why he chose acting as a career, he replied: 'I've been goofing around all my life. I thought I might as well get paid for it'

☆ *Jessica Lange* ☆

When she first met ballet dancer, Mikhail Baryshnikov, they spoke in French

A scene in which he kisses Jane Fonda in *The Electric Horseman* was shot forty-eight times, 7,500 feet of film were used for what became a twenty-second sequence. ☆ ☆ ☆

He's depressed about his chances of doing something for ecology. 'I get more coverage trying to sneak in and out of a restaurant,' he says.

He buys his 501s off the peg.

He denigrates his own myth by having pictures of himself on his toilet tissue at home.

'My kids are my best friends,' he says. 'They know what a clod I am. They know the person who's shy and awkward in social situations. They know the person who bumps into things, who opens the refrigerator door and says, "Where's the juice?" when it's right in front of him.'

Paul Newman calls him 'the smiling barracuda'. His father says he's a cross between a pussycat and Attila the Hun.

He calls acting 'a girl's job'. 'I act because it's the thing I do best,' he says, adding, 'I wish it was painting.'

He won an Oscar for directing *Ordinary People*. He didn't appear in that film, but still considers it one of his best performances because, 'I had to walk round the set like I knew what I was doing'.

If his children want extra pocket money they have to get part-time jobs.

☆ When a fan asked him once if he was Robert Redford
☆ he replied, 'Only when I'm alone.'
☆

His favourite four words are 'Once Upon A Time'.
Adulthood has never appealed much to this fifty-
something: 'Growing up is losing your freedom.'

Mickey Rourke

Somebody in a bar said to him once: 'You make too much money.' His reply? 'If they're dumb enough to offer it to me, I'm not dumb enough to turn it down.'

He professes to have no respect for the term 'actor': he would prefer it if they put 'animal' on his passport.

Of the much-hyped *9½ Weeks*, he now says, 'I had the impression we were going to break new territory on that movie, convey certain subtle and delicate things that go on between two people ... but I realize now that wouldn't have sold as many tickets as me humping Kim Basinger on a coffee table.'

These days, he claims, he's more interested in motor-cycles than sex.

His favourite director is currently-out-of-favour Michael Cimino, who worked with him on *Year of the Dragon*. After that movie wrapped, he said, 'If some-body would give me a piece of paper and say, "Just sign here and you work with Cimino for the next five years", I would sign it in two seconds.'

Life with his first wife Debra Feuer was difficult because, 'I'm the kind of guy who won't go to sleep till my eyes shut by themselves – I'm afraid I'm going to miss something.'

He spent $12,000 on suits for *9½ Weeks*, and $10,000 for 'flashy threads' for the earlier *Pope of Greenwich Village*, which was a box-office disaster.

☆
☆
☆

His favourite decades are the 50s and 80s: 'The 60s were a nightmare . . . and the 70s I don't remember.'

He likens acting to walking a greased tightrope without a safety net.

'I couldn't tell the truth,' he says, remembering his traumatic youth, 'if you hit me over the f***ing head with it.' He spent a lot of time 'hanging out at beaches popping downers' but got out of that rut the day he decided 'I didn't want to be a professional bad-ass'.

If he hadn't been an actor, he said once, he would have probably ended up as a criminal.

Goldie Hawn

She started dancing at the age of three.

She first came to fame as the 'ding-a-ling' in *Rowan and Martin's Laugh-In*. At that time, *Look* magazine described her as 'TV's dumbest and most delectable bonbon'.

She refused a 'casting couch' at the age of eighteen 'to go back to my little apartment and all the cockroaches'. (The mogul she rebuffed told her to 'go back home and marry a Jewish dentist, because you'll never get anywhere in this business'.)

She believes monogamy is impossible today – for both sexes. Her two marriages went on the rocks, she says, because her husbands couldn't handle the fact that she was making more money than they were.

She says she never wanted to be a star after she saw what happened to Elvis Presley. She met him once, on the set of the *Laugh-In*. He patted her on the head and said she reminded him of 'a newly-hatched chicken'.

Donald Zec said of her, 'If a brain hummed behind those dumbfounded eyes and that idiot giggle, the secret never leaked out.'

She concedes that film-making is a business and she a commodity. 'But so are Clint Eastwood and Barbra Streisand. And we all want the commodity to pay off. We want the three cherries.'

☆ People don't come up and ask her for her autograph
☆ any more, she insists: they come up and ask her to
☆ *giggle*.

She once drove a complete stranger who was in labour
to a hospital and stayed by her bedside for two hours.

'I'm a physical person in every way,' is her self-summation. 'Kurt Russell is my sexual object – we're basically
animals.'

She names her household pets after characters she's
played in films.

She'd like to direct eventually because the power of
the job appeals to her. When she asked a friend to
describe what directing entailed, he said, 'It's like
being in front of a moving train and running as fast as
you can.' She feels that's a pretty close description of
her own life thus far.

Paul Newman

His father was German/Jewish, his mother Hungarian.

Describing himself in high school he said, 'I was a short, scrawny, ninety-nine-pound kid who couldn't even qualify for the junior varsity football team.'

His original ambition was to be a pilot; it was quashed when he was discovered to be colour blind during a routine physical.

He stumbled into acting, he says, as a result of running away from what his father wanted him to do – run the family sporting goods store.

He had many odd jobs. One was selling encyclopedias ('I was really selling myself,' he says); another picking up golf balls and cleaning them for re-use.

His first film was called *The Silver Chalice*. One reviewer said, 'Newman delivers his lines with the emotional fervour of a Putnam train conductor announcing local stops.' When the film re-surfaced on TV some years later he took out an ad in the local daily papers to publicly apologize for his performance in it.

His first marriage failed. 'I feel guilty as hell about it,' he said after it broke up, 'and I'll carry that guilt for the rest of my life.' He subsequently married Joanne Woodward and is still with her twenty-five years on. 'Without her I'd be nowhere, nothing,' he claims.

☆
☆ He was nominated seven times for an Oscar before he
☆ finally won one for *The Color of Money*. He didn't
attend the ceremony.

He refuses to dye his hair because 'I don't have an adversarial relationship with the natural process of growing older'. Gulp.

He looks on people who ask to see his famed baby blue eyes as visual rapists. 'You work your butt off for fifteen years,' he said once, 'and all people can ask you is to take off your glasses.'

He fell in love with motor racing on the set of *Winning*, insisting on doing all the stunts himself. By the time he reached fifty he was one of the top drivers on the amateur circuit. 'If he had started in his twenties,' said a source, 'there's no doubt he'd have been a world champion.'

His son Scott was a stuntman before he overdosed in 1978. (He had a brief part in *The Towering Inferno*.) He felt a life-long inferiority complex that he couldn't emulate his father, which drove him to drunken binges and (subsequently) counselling.

He formed an enduring friendship with Robert Redford on the set of *Butch Cassidy and the Sundance Kid*. Redford once sent him a demolished Porsche. He retaliated by sending the Porsche back ... into the middle of Redford's dining-room. Redford showed no reaction.

He makes millions of dollars per year on his home-made salad dressing, most of which he gives to charity. 'I couldn't think of anything tackier than putting my name and reputation on a bottle of salad dressing, so I did it,' he says by way of explanation.

Peter O'Toole

His father was an inveterate gambler. 'When he'd come home from the track after a good day,' he remembers, 'the whole house would light up. It was fairyland. But when he lost, it was black. In our house it was either a wake or a wedding.'

He's been dogged by bad health all his life. During his childhood he had 'peritonitis, eye trouble, TB, the lot'. He had eight operations on his left eye in all, and also suffered from a stammer and a lisp. (The latter wasn't helped by the fact that his tongue had been sliced off by an over-zealous Swede swinging wildly with his foot during a rugby game at school.)

He's a natural left-hander but was forced to change at school. Each time he used his left hand he was beaten, and still has the scars to show for it.

He didn't attend school on a regular basis until he was eleven, and then stayed only two years.

He was an altar boy in youth, and calls the Mass his first 'performance'.

He insists he was brought up as a girl for the first twelve years of his life.

He describes himself as being, not from the working class, but 'the criminal class'.

He's always been superstitious. He never wears a watch, never carries a wallet and never takes house

☆
☆ keys with him. 'I just hope some bastard's in,' he says.
☆ (When they aren't, he's often been in the position of
explaining to police why he's breaking into his own
home.)

In 1974 he became uninsurable due to health problems. He thought he had cancer and prepared himself
to meet his Maker. He dropped down to nine stone in
weight, one doctor calling his dice with death a 'photo-
finish'. (Afterwards he was informed he would have to
give up excessive drinking.)

Because *The Bible* was directed by an Irishman (John
Huston) and featured himself and Richard Harris,
he said it should have been re-titled *Sodom and
Begorrah*, or *The Gospel According to Mick*.

He claims he doesn't have an Irish accent, nor does he
wish to acquire one. 'If you go around playing Irish
parts called Peter O'Toole,' he says, 'you'd have to
have red hair and carry a shillelagh.'

One of his acquaintances once said he was better able
to drive a camel than a car (alluding to his Oscar-winning role in *Lawrence of Arabia*). (He's written off at
least two cars.)

When Sam Spiegel said to him, 'I want you to play
Lawrence', he replied, 'Is it a speaking part?'

Someone once asked him to suggest another name for
the rhythm method of birth control and he suggested
Parenthood.

He has described Laurence Olivier as 'the most
charming, persuasive bastard ever to draw breath'.

In London, he says, you have to be a little mad to stay sane. Dublin in contrast, is a city where 'the only thing you can do is turn up the collar of your coat, pull your hat down over your eyes and walk straight through it; otherwise you're there forever'.

Liza Minnelli

Her mother Judy Garland once said of her: 'I think she decided to go into show business when she was an embryo.'

She once asked her father to drive 100 miles out of his way so she could change a dress she was wearing, and he duly did. 'Daddy, you really do understand me, don't you?' she said afterwards. She was four at the time.

By the time she was sixteen she had attended twelve different schools in the US and abroad.

She called herself the Queen of Ugly as a child.

Garland said of her early singing, 'My God, she's got a voice like chalk on a blackboard.'

Garland's threats of suicide ran into double figures before Liza reached her teens; eventually the latter invested in a stomach pump as a precaution.

She signed herself into the Betty Ford Clinic in 1984 suffering from valium and alcohol addiction. 'I'm sick and tired of being sick and tired,' she said, citing as causes of her problems a series of miscarriages, the deaths of her parents, two failed marriages and a topsy-turvy career. 'I was born with a disease in my blood,' she said later.

Her mother put severe demands on her mental health towards the end of her life. So much so that she once

left word with a doorman at her hotel that Garland not ☆
be allowed up to see her without it being previously ☆
arranged. ☆

When Garland invited her to her fifth wedding, she
said, 'I'm sorry I can't make it, Mama, but I promise
I'll come to your next one.'

Oprah Winfrey

She was so poor in her youth she never owned a store-bought dress.

She kept cockroaches as pets as a child.

'When I wake up and look in the mirror,' she says, 'I realize one of the reasons I don't own a handgun: I would have shot my thighs off years ago.'

A TV director once described her thus: 'Your hair's too long. Your eyes are too far apart, and your nose and chin are both too wide.'

'People think that because I'm in television,' she says, 'I have this great social life. Let me tell you, in the four years I spent in Baltimore I could count on my fingers the number of dates I had – and that includes the ones I paid for.'

After meeting Paul McCartney she said, 'Now I can die in peace.'

She was Oscar-nominated for her role in *The Color Purple*. In that film she played a character called Harpo – her own name reversed.

She once read a study that said that women not married by the age of forty have a greater chance of being killed by a terrorist than walking down the aisle.

She once had a goal of becoming a millionairess by the time she was thirty-two. Her attitude now is, 'You can only buy so many towels.'

'I want to be syndicated in very city known to
mankind,' she said in 1985.

☆
☆
☆

On one of her shows she interviewed a woman who
said she had been seduced by seven priests. Another,
on Satanic cults, heard a call from a fifteen-year-old
boy who said he had witnessed human sacrifices and
knew that one day he would have to sacrifice himself.

When the Ku Klux Klan appeared on her show she
asked them if they'd be interested in having lunch
afterwards.

She once told Chris Anderson of *Good Housekeeping*:
'The best place to find single men these days is the
frozen-food section of the supermarket, around 7 pm.'

☆
☆
☆

Sylvester Stallone

As a youth he developed a penchant for urinating into plug sockets. At other times he was to be found jumping off roofs with an umbrella *à la* Superman.

By the age of sixteen he had passed through twelve schools – mostly with dire academic results.

When he was seventeen his mother gave him a dollar to read Errol Flynn's *My Wicked, Wicked Ways*. He was happy to oblige.

He claims he learned acting before a mirror – on the 'If I can convince myself, I can convince anyone' style of thinking.

He failed his first audition because the director (Sal Mineo) said he wasn't intimidating enough. He countered that charge by intimidating Mineo! (The latter conceded he *could* be frightening, but still didn't give him the part.)

He wrote all the Rocky films, and directed three of them. His co-star in the first one, Talia Shire, described him as an intellectual caveman. Another colleague was less kind, saying 'He's become such a bastard even his dog turned on him and bit him.'

'The films I did in the 80s,' he says, commenting on the upsurge of screen violence, 'compared to what I've already seen in the 90s, were like walks in the park. In *Rambo* it was bullet, hit, gone. Not it's bullet, hit, explosion ... and people turning into human wallpaper. As regards the myth that everything in the 90s is going back to family-oriented films – ha ha. You know, let's just see, like Rudolph the Red-Nosed Reindeer with a Kalashnikov.'

Brigitte Nielson started sending him fan letters when she was eleven.

When they were dating, each had the other's name tattooed on their buttocks amid small clusters of flowers.

His first son by his first wife is autistic.

After Reagan saw *Rambo* he said, apropos the US hostages held in the Lebanon, 'I now know what to do the next time this happens.'

When he was unable to afford to go to a laundrette in his struggling days, he used to shower in his clothes.

His least favourite film is *Rhinestone*. He described the studio's attempt to promote it as giving away free rides on the Titanic.

At his wedding to Brigitte Nielson he parodied himself by saying, 'Wid dis ring I dee wed.'

A month after Nielson moved in with him she was cast as the second female lead of *Rocky IV*. (She deserted a husband and son in Denmark to be with him.)

An over-strenuous workout for *Rocky II* left him with a ripped *pectoralis major*, which meant an operation and 156 stitches. 'The fight sequence,' he said later, 'was choreographed by the Marquis de Sade.'

☆ *War and Peace,* he feels, is too long – but it would make
☆ a great novelette.
☆

He swears he'd never run for office. 'Other people
have skeletons in their closet – I have a graveyard!'

Robert de Niro

His first part was as a cowardly lion in a school version of *The Wizard of Oz*.

He was only paid $50 for his first screen role. (Compare that to $1½ million for the eleven days he spent on the set of *The Untouchables*.)

When he was researching the role of Travis Bickle in *Taxi Driver*, he cruised the streets of New York in a yellow cab. One day a passenger said to him, 'You're the actor, aren't you? Guess it's hard to find steady work.' (The psychopathic John Hinckley said he was inspired by this role – he saw the movie fifteen times – to attempt to assassinate the then president, Ronald Reagan, and to impress de Niro's co-star in the movie, Jodie Foster.)

Jake La Motta, the boxer he portrayed in his Oscar-winning role in *Raging Bull*, said he could have made it into the top twenty middleweights in real life, so impressive was his sparring with him. (He knocked La Motta's teeth out during one session, the latter billing the film company $4,000 for the dental charges.) De Niro put on sixty pounds for the role. 'I ate and drank twenty-four hours a day,' he said later. 'Beer, milk and so on. You can't imagine what kind of torture it was. I couldn't breathe no more, I couldn't even change my shoes.' (After the film was wrapped he used to look at his thirty-pound son in the bathroom and think: I have to lose two of him.)

☆ For the part of Al Capone in *The Untouchables*,
☆ he tracked down Capone's underwear tailor to have
☆ identical pairs of the mobster's favourite silk underpants made. (He also spent days with the latter's cigar
makers before deciding which ones to smoke.)

He hung around with real-life bounty hunters to pre-
pare himself for playing one of the same in the comedy
Midnight Run, even going so far as to make some
arrests. He wore a bullet-proof vest at all times, and
signed a contract absolving the police of culpability if
he got killed in action.

Both of his parents were painters.

Here's his philosophy of acting: 'To be able to be oneself straight on is hard. Actors always feel that they
have to *do* something. If they're not doing anything,
they're not doing enough. But the fact that they're
doing nothing is maybe all they have to do.' So now
you know.

He claims he falls asleep watching himself on TV.

He learned the entire Latin Mass by heart before playing a priest in *True Confessions*.

He rehearsed the part of the man suffering from sleeping sickness in *Awakenings* in an incontinence nappy –
and actually developed real facial tremors during the
shooting of that movie.

He refused the part of Jesus in *The Last Temptation of
Christ* because he said there was no way he could
research it.

When he was asked what the chief reward of success was, he said, 'You get a better table at restaurants.'

One of the stipulations of recent interviews is that the words Naomi and Campbell can't be used in close proximity to one another.

Shelley Winters, a former co-star, says of him: 'He could force his hair to curl on command if he wanted to.'

When Jerry Lewis asked him to dinner one night during the filming of *King of Comedy* he demurred. 'Listen Jerry,' he said, 'you better know where I'm coming from. I'm going to want to *kill* you in the picture. I certainly don't want to have dinner with you.' So he didn't.

Jodie Foster

She began her acting career at the age of three when she played the leading baby in a Coppertone advertisement.

She was the main financial supporter of her family before she could write.

She was only eighteen when ex-disc jockey John Hinckley tried to assassinate Ronald Reagan as a testament to his obsessive fascination for her. It was later revealed that he had seen *Taxi Driver*, in which she plays a twelve-year-old hooker, befriended by a character who stalks a presidential candidate, no less than fifteen times. (He eventually reached a point where he believed he *was* the eponymous driver.)

Before the assassination attempt, Hinckley sent her 100 poems and love letters, twice visiting Yale (where she was then studying) and hand-delivering his *billets doux* to her dormitory.

The following year she discovered a Hinckley clone following her on the same campus, on one occasion attending a play she was acting in, with a loaded gun in his pocket. She said afterwards of that phase of her life: 'In a time of crisis you resort to strengths you'd never dreamed you owned, like frantic mothers lifting their children from under two-ton trucks. The will to survive is stronger than any emotion.'

Her ideal day, she claims, consists of sitting round the house in her pajamas . . . and laughing hysterically at very very bad TV shows. (Sometimes, she says, she doesn't get out of bed for a week.)

She tries to live a spartan lifestyle, at least by Hollywood standards. 'I'd rather die,' she says, 'than have thirty paintings in my house that are worth $7 million each.' She admits, however, to a love of pots and pans.

Asked what she would like to be remembered for, she said it wouldn't be her acting or even directing. 'No, it's the fact that I make a really mean leek vinaigrette.'

☆
☆
☆

Clint Eastwood

When he was twenty, a plane he was travelling in crashed into the sea, landing in a pool of jellyfish. He had to swim for his life, but this didn't bother him as much as the five-mile hike in wet clothing to the nearest highway.

In early film roles – he made ten movies before *A Fistful of Dollars* – he says he was usually the lab technician who says, 'Doctor, here are the X-rays.' And the doctor would say, 'Get lost, kid.' And that would be the end of it.

Universal eventually signed him as a contract player, which is a little lower than working in the mail room.

His general philosophy of acting is that of his old drama coach: Don't just do something, stand there.

Judith Crist, a film critic, said of *The Beguiled*: 'This film is tailored exclusively for sadists and woman-haters. Its thesis is that women will calmly kill any man who denies them sexual satisfaction. And yet this excrescence is rated R. The family that likes to vomit together can do it here.'

He once fired a shot over a fan's head when she refused to leave the set of one of his films fast enough.

He says he got where he is today without studio packaging: 'I never had my picture taken kissing my dog as I got off a plane, or any of that crap.'

One of his first actions as Mayor of Carmel was to outlaw skateboards.

He once described himself as a loner, a screw-up and a bum.

He agrees that marriages are made in heaven. But so are thunder and lightning.

Basically he believes that women are superior to men. His logic? You see a lot of smart men with bimbos, but you don't see a lot of smart women with dumb guys.

He's unfazed by his general reputation for misogyny. 'I was criticized for knocking the leading lady through a window in *Play Misty For Me*. But the point was, she was trying to put a knife through my forehead.'

He spent thirteen years with Sondra Locke, but in April 1989 she was served with a court order to vacate the premises they shared. In retaliation, she slapped him with a $35 million palimony lawsuit. The latter was particularly unusual because she was married to another man right through their relationship!

His idea of a religious experience is 'standing on Half Dome looking down into Yosemite Valley.'

☆
☆
☆

Jessica Lange

She moved house twelve times before she left high school.

She had a whirlwind romance with hippie-cum-astrology buff Paco Grande in the late 60s, marrying him in 1970, while the sun was still in Leo. 'How could a marriage like that fail?' she said afterwards. But it did.

Her lifestyle with Grande was unconventional, to say the least. While travelling with him one day in his Cadillac, it blew up. 'So we got out, closed the doors, and left it burning in the middle of the street.'

When she first met ballet dancer Mikhail Baryshnikov they spoke in French.

Her relationship to Sam Shepard remains deeply romantic. Somebody who spotted them at a restaurant some time ago said, 'They were literally *attached* to each other. I don't think a lot of eating was going on, because her mouth was constantly full of his hand.'

Shepard, she says, is the first totally monogamous relationship she's had since the early 80s.

Shepard dug her father's grave when the latter died.

She sometimes feels like a borderline schizophrenic because depression hits her so hard. 'There are times I feel so close to the edge I could easily tip over. If it weren't for the kids, I could very well be gone – emotionally *and* physically.'

She says that every man she's ever been attracted to has been a ladies' man. ☆ ☆ ☆

She refuses to live in LA, even if it would help her career. Nor does she envy the Julia Roberts of the world, saying: 'I'd hate to be talking to an agent every day at twenty-five.'

She started filming *King Kong* in the month of June, but the Gentle Giant himself didn't show up until August. 'Most of the time I was playing to a spot on the ceiling,' she said.

Besides Shepard, she shares her bed with four dogs.

When asked what she'd like engraved on her head-stone, she said, 'Just one word – Mother.'

Dustin Hoffman

His first memory is of having his hands tied to the side of the crib so he couldn't bite his nails. (It didn't work, and he still does.)

'A lustful nerd' is how he describes himself at high school.

In his early days, he went five times a week to his analyst – at $200 a session.

After *The Graduate* made him an overnight sensation, he saw his name in lights on a billboard and thought: 'That person up there is more successful than me. He's working, and I'm not.' (After he auditioned for that part, director Mel Brooks told him blithely, 'You're not going to get it because you're an ugly little rat.')

He believes art is so important you should be allowed to sell out your mother to make it good.

He claims he sometimes gets so wrapped up in his screen character he forgets his true identity.

When he played Lenny Bruce in *Lenny* he got an Oscar nomination for the very words Bruce himself, in a previous era, was arrested for.

The key to the 121-year-old man he played in *Little Big Man*, he says, 'was that he hadn't had a decent bowel movement in forty-six years'.

There was a moment during the shooting of *Midnight Cowboy* where he gave so much energy to Ratso's coughing, he fell down on the street throwing up. (His co-star Jon Voight later commented: 'There's no way I can upstage vomit.')

He once described movie-making as 'painting a picture on a railroad track with the train getting closer'.

When shooting *The Graduate*, they had to film all the pool scenes underwater, because that's the only way he could swim.

Temperamental clashes on film sets don't bother him if the end product is worth it. 'I'd work with Yasser Arafat,' he claims, 'if he gave me script control.'

He claims he's never been in a fistfight in his life.

He says he turned down the title role of *Rambo*, preferring to make his living playing wimps.

He believes a good review from a critic is only a stay of execution.

He thinks the orgasm has replaced God in contemporary sociology.

He has the happy knack of convincing himself he's always going to live to be double the age he is at any given time.

Some wag once suggested he should have won the Best Actress Award for *Tootsie*.

He regards himself as liberal, to a point: 'If one of my children came to me and said, "I'm gay," I'd say, "Fine, I hope you find a nice boyfriend." If one said they were lesbian I'd say the same thing. But if one said they wanted to be a movie critic, I'd say, "Let's sit down and talk about it." '

Barbra Streisand

She was born in a poor district of Brooklyn, a place she described later as being 'boredom, baseball and bad breath'.

She was only fifteen months old when her thirty-four-year-old father died of a cerebral haemorrhage. She was brought up by an elderly grandmother until she was seven, at which time her mother re-married.

Her first doll, she claims, was a hot water bottle.

She went to school in 'a place where they train you to wed a dentist'.

She describes herself in youth as 'anaemic, bullied . . . and ugly'.

Her first performance was as a chocolate chip cookie.

She gave up smoking at thirteen because she could do it at school and nobody cared.

In her Oriental period, she let her fingernails grow to Fu-Manchu length.

She claims to have been a personality before she was a person.

She once defined success as 'having ten honeydew melons and only eating the top of each one'.

Jon Franklin once asked her how much she would

☆
☆
☆

charge to haunt him. She wasn't amused.

After she kissed Omar Sharif in *Funny Girl* (he's Egyptian and she's Jewish) she said, 'You think Cairo's upset? You should have seen the letter from my Aunt Rose!'

As far back as 1968 she made The Worst Dressed Women list, one designer describing her as a flower child gone to seed in the cabbage patch.

When she became mega after *Funny Girl* she said, 'There's nothing better than to know I can be taking a bath at home and at the same time someone is watching me in Brazil.'

She says she's plagued by insecurities. 'Outside I look okay, but deep down I'm a definite basket case.'

She's reputed to be worth between $70 and $80 million.

'When I'm not performing,' she said once, 'I don't think I have a definite personality. In fact I think maybe I'm nothing.'

On stage, things make sense, she feels – but in life they don't.

Being a celebrity is a no-win situation, she says: 'If you get along with your co-star you're having an affair; if you don't, you're having a feud.'

Every time she gets a role offer, she fantasizes about Marlon Brando playing opposite her.

☆ Her biggest nightmare is driving home and getting sick
☆ in transit, with people around her saying, 'Hey, you
☆ look like . . .' as she pleads for help. Then she dies . . .
and they're still wondering if she's Barbra Streisand.

Robin Williams

His mother and father were always working, he says, 'so I was basically raised by the maid.'

He admits he wasn't an ideal husband to his first wife Valerie: 'I'd been running round doing all sorts of things – drink, drugs, several affairs. I was a bad boy.' (He says he stopped drinking after waking up once under his car . . . with the keys in his ear.)

He defines cocaine now as 'God's way of telling you you're making too much money'.

He claims he gets his sense of humour from his mother, who inherited it from *her* mother. 'When I was young, both of them used to recite nasty poems to me. There's a lot of happy madness that's been passed down.'

He feels he's most creative when he's not in charge of things. Because the ego locks the muse.

He defines success as a three-piece suit. That's the three-piece *law* suit.

In a *Playboy* interview in 1982 he said, 'The French are going one better than the Americans with their Michelin bomb: it's only going to destroy restaurants under four stars.'

Corpsing on stage he likens to 'being circumcised in the Grand Canyon'.

☆
☆
☆
He liked the soft Scottish accent he developed for the gender-bending role of *Mrs Doubtfire* because you could say 'Fuck off' and it came across as 'Ooh, bless you dear'. Donning the copious robes of that lady he described as 'like being in the world's largest condom'.

The first time he tried organic wheat bread, he thought he was chewing on roofing material.

He describes his brand of comedy as not dissimilar to emotional hang-gliding.

He likes to call his children names with a Z in them, like Zachary and Zelda; his present wife, Marsha Garces, was Zachary's former nanny.

He says he wouldn't like to become a director because, if he criticized something an actor did, the latter could say, 'Who are you to talk – what about *Popeye*?' . . . and he would be stumped for an answer.

Sigourney Weaver

★

Her real name is Susan. The Sigourney she picked up from a character in *The Great Gatsby* . . . who never appears on screen. She chose it because it was 'long and curvy'.

She refuses to 'go' Hollywood. Those who do, she says, 'usually end up floating round the ozone layer and having a lot of face-lifts'.

She turned down, wait for it, *Fatal Attraction*, *Body Heat* and *9½ Weeks*.

For *Alien 3* she earned $2½ million, and also three per cent of the gross; compare that to the 'measly' $18,000 she was paid for the original *Alien*.

Early drama teachers described her as 'uncastable' because of her height. (She's six foot.) On one occasion a producer was reluctant to use her in a role because she was taller than the leading man. 'Why don't I paint a pair of shoes on my feet and I'll play the role barefoot?' she suggested.

A clairvoyant once advised her not to marry before she reached thirty-five; she went to the altar a mere week before her thirty-fifth birthday.

Her debut role was a cameo in Woody Allen's *Annie Hall*. 'Unless you know my raincoat, you'll miss me,' she says of the tiny part.

Her original ambition was to be a marine biologist.

☆ After *Alien* she said, 'Just call me Rambolina.'
☆
☆ *The Year of Living Dangerously* proved an apt movie title for her, her life being threatened by Muslim extremists, who subsequently forced Peter Weir to move location shooting away from Manila.

She once did a mock-interview where the following question/answer session took place:

Q. How did you get the leading role in *Alien*?
A. I slept with the director.
Q. And *Eyewitness*?
A. I slept with the director and the writer and crew.
Q. And *The Year of Living Dangerously*?
A. I slept with the Australian consulate.

'Maternity clothes are all so awful,' she told *You* magazine in 1989. 'If I wear Laura Ashley stuff, being so tall, it makes me look like a kindergarten child in time warp.'

One of the prices of fame, she feels, is: 'You have to be charming to strangers who grow angry and scream at you because they think you owe them more than a performance.'

Filming *Gorillas in the Mist* proved even more hazardous than *The Year of Living Dangerously*. As she puts it herself, 'When you have 400 pounds of pissed-off gorilla inching up on you, you start seeing your life flash by.'

Michael Caine

He was born Maurice Joseph Micklewhite. When he joined Actor's Equity he changed that to Michael Scott, but they already had a Michael Scott on their books so he had to change again. Caine came from *The Caine Mutiny*, which he spotted on a billboard through a cluster of trees. 'I could have been Michael 101 Dalmations if the trees had been in a different place,' he said afterwards.

When he was young he was called Old Snake Eyes because he never blinked. Such a trait came in useful as an actor, he claims.

In his first play he played a robot. A critic in the *South London Press* wrote, 'Mr Caine was very convincing as a robot.'

He was so nervous in his first TV performance that he forgot his lines . . . all three of them.

He didn't think he was actor material 'until I saw van Johnson had freckles just like me.'

He said yes to *Alfie* before he got to page two of the script. After the film made him famous he said, 'I've had every man in the world tell me he's Alfie, from Ravi Shankar to the chief of Customs in Taiwan.'

A critic said of *Harry and Walter Go To New York*: 'It looks as if it was photographed by the kind of illumination you find in vandalized telephone kiosks.'

☆
☆
☆
He was nervous played a transvestite in *Dressed To Kill* ... in case he got to *like* it. When the film was shown in Bradford, where the Yorkshire Ripper lived, women threw pig's blood at the screen, imagining its violence had spurred that man into action.

John Wayne once gave him a valuable piece of acting advice: 'If you want to last in this business, kid, talk low, talk slow – and don't say too damn much.'

He loves giving interviews – even to the *Poultry Farmers' Weekly Gazette*.

He says he'd prefer to go mad than see a psychiatrist.

He doesn't think God belongs to any religion.

People who break their word in Japan kill themselves, he says, 'but people who break their word in Hollywood kill *you*'.

After a week working on *Ashanti*, the fired the leading lady, the director, the art director and the editor. 'So I had a faint inkling we might be on to a spotty project there.'

Before he gave his famous homosexual screen kiss to Christopher Reeve in *Deathtrap*, he said to him, 'If you open your mouth I'll kill you.' The actors downed a bottle of brandy to get up courage to do the scene. He also said, 'If you stick your tongue out I'm going to put my leg up backwards the way Doris Day used to do.'

His salary for Neil Jordan's *Mona Lisa* was, he says, 'two bob and a lollipop.'

He won an Oscar for *Hannah and Her Sisters*, though he was only on the set four weeks.

Success is all a matter of fashion, he believes: 'If you're hot they'll alter the part from a black midget for you; but if you're cold it's a case of, "We're making *The Michael Caine Story*, but we're afraid you're too tall for it".'

He feeds guppies to the kingfishers that live in his grounds.

Women still put pieces of paper into his pocket with their phone numbers on them, he insists.

His philosophy of acting is: 'I'm getting paid for something I would do for nothing. You can't beat that!'

Madonna

Members of her family call her 'The Mouth'.

She married Sean Penn on her twenty-sixth birthday.

She runs five miles every day.

She's never released a single with more than three words in the title because she thinks it's unlucky.

She remains unfazed about media allegations concerning her sexuality, commenting, 'They used to say I was an easy lay, a slut, a sex bomb, or even Marlene Dietrich's daughter. I'd rather say I'm more a hyperactive adult.'

She doesn't like men who are afraid of their femininity.

Material Girl or not, she's made over $200 million in the past five years. She is currently said to be worth seven times that overall.

She met Warren Beatty on her first date with Sean Penn.

'Drinking martinis is about as out of control as I get,' she said once.

When she was young, her father insisted she go to church every morning before school.

She got her first kiss in a convent. In her teens she was called 'nympho' by the boys she knew, and 'slut' by the girls. She lost her virginity in the back of a Cadillac, she claims, 'as a career move.'

When she was a child she was asked what she wanted to do after she grew up and she replied, 'Rule the world.'

One biographer said of her: 'She likes everything neat, like her closets. She's a symbol of the Filofax generation. Her appointments and her phone calls are scheduled. She knows it's close to an obsession, like her exercise routine, but she still won't change. She exercises to stop being depressed, and if she didn't exercise she'd be depressed about not exercising.'

She's only taken three holidays in the last ten years – and was bored by the second day of each.

She finds nuns sexy, particularly because they wear no make-up.

She was born only one day apart from her ex-husband Sean Penn, and on the same day as Elvis Presley died. In a sense, she feels his spirit lives on in her body, giving her the inspiration to perform.

Her views on celebrity status? 'You don't understand being hugely famous until it happens – and then it's too late to decide if you want it or not.'

She once dyed her hair a different colour for every day of the week.

Globally she's sold seventy-five million albums, to date.

Sex isn't dirty, she claims, if you have a bath after it.

The soft side of her nature, on the contrary, causes her to cry every time she sees *The Wizard of Oz*.

☆
☆ She's rumoured to have had a lesbian affair with her
☆ friend Sandra Bernhard, and she hasn't denied it: 'If it
makes people feel better to think I slept with her, then
they can think it. And if it makes them feel safer to
think I didn't, then that's okay too.'

She's surprised to have lived past thirty, having imagined she'd die at the same age as her mother.

A reviewer of her movie bomb *Who's That Girl?* said of her appearance in that film: 'She's been made up and costumed to look like an aspiring bag lady with the skin of a pneumonia victim.'

Some psychics have told her that she's the reincarnation of Marilyn Monroe.

A friend once asked her to look after her pet poodles while she was away. When she came back she found one of them had been spray-painted pink and the other orange.

She's bought a burial plot next to Marilyn Monroe so they can be together for ever.

She began her career living out of rubbish bins in New York, existing mainly on popcorn and deserted McDonald's french fries.

Her mother didn't allow her to use tampons because she felt they were like having sex.

Warren Beatty said of her that she doesn't see any point to existing unless there's a camera trained on her somewhere.

☆
☆
☆

Her favourite activity at parties is talking to the butler and the janitors. Or so she says . . .

Her feminist thesis: Guys get to do everything. They get to be altar boys, they get to stay out late, take off their shirts in the summer. They even get to pee standing up . . .

When she was in the sixth grade she had an erotic dream wherein she was kissed by Robert Redford. 'But it hasn't come true,' she adds, morosely.

From when she was very young, she says, 'I knew that being a girl and being charming in a feminine sort of way could get me a lot of things, and I milked it for everything I could.'

When Shirley MacLaine was asked how easy it would be to have her for a sister-in-law (she was dating Warren Beatty at the time) she replied, 'As easy as it would be for me to nail a custard pie to the wall.'

Macho guys don't go for her, she claims – because they're frightened of their femininity.

She was sacked from her waitressing job at Dunkin' Donuts – for squirting jam over a customer.

On a shopping spree in Manhattan once, she spent £8,000 on shoes.

Despite her superstar status, she says, she's been known to wash the occasional dish and make the occasional bed. And sometimes, just sometimes, driving around in her megabucks cars, she thinks: 'God, I'm just a girl from Michigan.'

Al Pacino

He says 'fuck' 183 times in *Scarface*. Joan Collins quipped: 'That's more than most people get in a lifetime.'

He once described himself as a Taurus/Aries cusp, with a moon in Sagittarius and a cow in Kansas.

While trying to get into the part of a policeman in *Serpico*, he made a citizen's arrest.

After he played *Richard II*, he found himself still walking round with a limp all day: 'The body doesn't know a role is over until the mind tells it.'

'I've lived with women since I've been sixteen,' he says – and they've all been actresses. 'When I was young,' he claims, 'I'd see an attractive girl on the street and start to follow her. Sometimes I'd catch up with her, we'd look at each other, and before long we'd be making out.'

He was paid $35,000 for *Godfather I*. That figure swelled to $600,000 for the sequel two years later, plus a percentage of the gross.

Ellen Barkin said 'yes' to the script of *Sea of Love* before she even read it, because he was to be her co-star.

One critic wrote of the ill-fated *Revolution*: 'His first speech in the film is spoken as if he were a ventriloquist.' Another said it was so idiotic 'it makes me wonder if it wasn't chewed to bits in the editing lab by a gang of mice ... Kids staging a Fourth of July pageant couldn't come up with anything this hilariously bad.'

He agrees with Laurence Olivier that the best thing about the theatre is the drink after the show. 'Whiskey is very under-rated. I know, because I've been to psychoanalysts and they didn't calm me down as much as a good belt.'

His overall ambition is to get to the point in acting 'where you don't have to act. When you get the urge to act,' he once told a female co-star, 'lie down and wait for it to pass.' She said it was the best piece of advice she had ever received.

James Woods said of *Scarface*: 'I'm all for any movie where the lead character keeps a grenade-launcher in the living-room.'

☆
☆
☆

Marlon Brando

★

Both of his parents were alcoholics.

His first professional biography read: 'Born in Calcutta, India, but left there at six months of age.'

He broke his nose during a boxing session with Jack Palance, but declined to have it re-set because he felt he was too pretty.

Harry Cohn liked him so much he once said he would cast him 'reading a telephone book'.

He has described rape as 'assault with a friendly weapon'.

He has this to say of fame in general: 'You're just sitting on a pile of candy gathering thick layers of crust.'

He once rebuffed a potential biographer by telling him that his proposed work would be 'about as beneficial to posterity as frozen monkey vomit'.

Apropos his legendary reputation with women, Hedda Hopper commented: 'He's just plain clumsy, and that's the truth. If he weren't a film star, he wouldn't get to first base.'

His son Christian is currently serving a ten-year jail sentence for the killing of his sister Cheyenne's boyfriend, Dag Drollet. Brando describes him as a boy who was a basket case throughout his youth, claiming the boy's mother (Anna Kashfi) often threatened to kill him in front of the boy.

He was so anxious to land the part of Don Corleone in *The Godfather* in 1970 that he underwent the relative ignominy of a screen test for the role – his first since 1946.

James Caan, his co-star in *The Godfather*, says, 'Anyone of my generation who says he hasn't "done" Brando is lying.' After *On the Waterfront* was released, Albert Finney says there were '150 guys outside RADA doing Brando imitations'.

Peter Evans described him as 'the man who made a lot of scratch from an itch'.

After *Superman*, James Woods said, 'The greatest screen actor in the history of the cinema running around with white hair in a Krypton suit – there's gotta be something wrong with that.'

Elia Kazan, who directed him in *On the Waterfront* said his performance in that film was the greatest he ever saw in his life.

He went to Hollywood from Broadway, he said, because he didn't have the moral courage to refuse the money.

He once defined an actor as 'a guy who, if you ain't talkin' about him, he ain't listenin''.

He has no respect for the profession in general. 'It's the expression of a neurotic impulse,' he says, adding, 'It's a bum's life. You get paid for doing nothing and it means nothing. It's a fundamentally childish thing to pursue. Quitting acting – that's the sign of maturity.'

☆ Bernardo Bertolucci, who directed him in *Last Tango*
☆ *in Paris*, described him as 'an angel of a man, a mon-
☆ ster of an actor'.

When Al Pacino was nervous going into a take with
him for *The Godfather*, he explained his reason to the
director: 'I'm acting with God, that's why.' (The first
time Pacino saw *On the Waterfront*, he said he couldn't
move – he was glued to the seat.)

He spent his early thespian years in a brownstone
apartment in New York, spending his time dropping
paper bags full of water onto passersby, playing bongo
drums in the small hours . . . and raising a pet raccoon.

He told Truman Capote in an intimate interview once:
'My mother was everything to me, a whole world. I used
to come home from school but she wouldn't be there
and there'd be nothing in the ice box. Then the telephone would ring and it would be somebody calling
from a bar to pick her up. Then one day I didn't care any
more. She was there in a room holding on to me and I let
her fall. I couldn't take it any more, watching her break
apart like a piece of porcelain. I stepped right over her.
I was indifferent. Since then I've been indifferent.'

His son Christian, he says, has been an alcoholic since
the age of fourteen.

In the recent Christopher Columbus movie *1492* he
wanted Columbus portrayed as the true villain he was: a
man directly responsible for the first wave of genocidal
obliteration of the native peoples of North America.
He said of *Last Tango*: 'I don't think Bertolucci knew
what the film was about. I didn't either. He went
around telling everyone it was about his prick.'

He finds he gets fanatically interested in every project ☆
he undertakes . . . for about seven minutes. ☆
☆

He lists his main influences as Schopenhauer, James
Joyce 'and my aunt Minnie'.

His passport lists him as, not Actor, but 'Shepherd'.

Acting, he says, has 'nothing whatsoever to do with
anything important. You haven't the slightest idea of
what you're doing. You walk in and do a scene based
on what you thought up in the bathtub.'

A former girlfriend describes him like this: 'He has the
face of a poet, and the body of an animal; he's a walking hormone factory.'

At the moment, he claims to be malingering under a
desperate melancholy. 'Here I am,' he says, 'a balding,
middle-aged failure. I feel a fraud when I act. I've tried
everything – fucking, drinking, work. None of it means
anything now.'

He says this about love: 'If it should die in me, it would
be the end. It doesn't matter if I have almost never
been happy with a woman, nor does it matter that
with every woman, my relationship has ended up in
nothing. I face love every time as a necessary good or
a necessary evil. Sometimes I even approach love and
sex with boredom. But I must make love and give love,
whatever the price. It is a matter of life and death.'

When he refused his Oscar for *The Godfather* on prin-
ciple, a studio executive commented: 'I'm sick of these
bleeding-hearted liberals who grow fat on the capital-
ism they despise.'

☆
☆   In 1979 his weight swelled up to 300 pounds. One night
☆   a friend found him haemorrhaging on a pillow,
    attributing the incident to the fact that he had eaten an
    entire gallon of ice cream at a sitting.

Unable to memorize screen lines in recent years, he
developed a system whereby he had people read them
to him through wires leading into a hearing aid.

'Death and old age,' he says, 'are events which I accept
and await with all feasible serenity. To a certain extent,
at times I make of them the purpose of living. I work
towards the point at which I can accept them with
equanimity.'

Roman Polanski

He was removed from kindergarten after the first day, for using an obscenity.

During the shooting of *Chinatown*, he threw a television set through a trailer window when Jack Nicholson insisted on looking at a basketball match rather than doing a take. Polanski did a cameo scene in that film – which Nicholson directed!

When he was told an actress he was planning to use for a scene had fainted, he said, 'Well, tell her to *un*faint.'

One critic said, '*Tess* is adequate only as a documentary about nineteenth-century dairy farming.'

The script for his *Repulsion* was completed in seventeen days.

Since Sharon Tate was murdered by the Charles Manson gang, he's admitted he could never again give himself to one woman in a permanent relationship, 'no matter how beautiful, bright, easy-going, good-natured or attuned to my moods', because any emotional attachment carries the risk of another heartbreak. (Her death also shattered any *religious* faith he had: 'It reinforced my faith in the absurd.')

The notion of dying with a healthy bank balance is repugnant to him.

Richard Gere

In 1976, when he was waiting on tables in Greenwich Village, he went up to a table at which Robert de Niro – fresh from the huge success of *Taxi Driver* – sat sipping a coffee. 'Man,' he said, pointing his finger at the star, 'someday I'm going to be as famous as you are.'

He is credited with organizing the casting of the female lead in 1983's *Breathless* all by himself. In the nude. As were all the interviewees . . .

His wife – supermodel Cindy Crawford – is seventeen years his junior.

He converted to Buddhism when he was twenty-four, and later helped found the Tibet House in New York City, a non-profit centre designed to campaign for the liberation of Tibet. Studying the writings of the Dalai Lama, he says, has helped him to stop being selfish and inner-directed. 'All our daily lives', he says rather Lama-esquely, 'the thing we call reality is just an expression of the spirit.'

The beach house he bought with Cindy Crawford knocked him back a cool $2,500,000. Considering that she earns in the region of $6 million a year, even without him, though, it's hardly extravagant.

Asked recently about her influence on him, he conceded: 'She's stopped me swearing at photographers.'

Christopher Reeve said of him: 'He plays the kind of guy who says to a woman, "I wanna get laid, and you're gonna get laid whether you like it or not." I'm the kind of guy who says, "Please."'

Harrison Ford

He went into movies, he says, to meet girls, and to qualify for health insurance.

He didn't know whether to start his career on the east or west coast, so he flipped a coin. It came up New York . . . so he flipped it again.

'Failures are inevitable,' he says, 'but unfortunately, in film, they live for ever. And they're forty-foot wide and twenty-foot high.'

He describes himself as 'an ordinary creaky set of bones that has to work hard to get in shape for a film'.

Here's how he described his attitude to his ground-breaking movie, *Star Wars*: 'I had a difficult time with lines like, "It'll take a mega-second for the nava computer to calculate the coordinates." You feel silly shooting guns that make no sound and destroying battleships you're unable to see because the special effects won't be done for months.'

Carrie Fisher says he's the type of guy who doesn't see much difference between fixing a kid's hurt finger to saving a galaxy.

If he finds the word 'handsome' in a script, he runs away from it.

The day before he started shooting *Raiders of the Lost Ark*, it was discovered that the serum they were using to treat cobra bites – which can paralyze a person in

☆
☆ thirty seconds – was out of date. Replacement stock
☆ had to be flown in from Paris.

He doesn't believe in the current spate of sex in movies. 'People don't want to see how the plumbing works,' he says.

'Our culture's interest in actors' personal lives,' he once said, 'is just mythicalization and bullshit.'

A recluse of Garboesque proportions, he says you'd only find him in a disco 'if I died and didn't go to heaven.'

Anthony Hopkins

He called Shirley MacLaine 'the most obnoxious actress I've ever worked with' after, he claimed, she was bitchy with him on the set of *A Change of Seasons*.

After *The Silence of the Lambs*, he says he could hardly stop at traffic lights without someone rolling down the window and asking him, 'Had your dinner yet, Hannibal?'

When he played a ventriloquist in *Magic* he found it helpful to treat his dummy as a human being. When researching the role, he heard of a man who used to book his dummy into a separate hotel room when they toured.

All his life, he says, he's felt 'genetically maladjusted'. 'I've always felt I've got this missing gene. I just wanted to be off this bloody planet. I had this notion that there was some special book they passed out at birth and I'd been missed.'

His relationship to the opposite sex, he claims, is complex: 'I'm absurdly shy of women so I pretend I don't like them. Then people think I'm arrogant.'

The art of acting, he once said, is not to act.

He says of his alcohol-riddled past: 'I thought it was clever to drink people under the table, but I wasn't happy. I was a pain in the arse really.'

☆ He says he had some hallucinogenic and/or quasi-
☆ religious experiences after drinking Tequila Sunrises.
☆ On one occasion he thought he was John the Baptist
talking to the sea, and the sea talked back.

A friend once gave him a present of a teddy bear carrying a gun, in order to make him aware of his own
Jekyll and Hyde behavioural patterns.

When he was young he was able to hypnotize people
by pulling their ear lobes.

He doesn't enjoy working with horses in films, describing them as 'nightmares on four legs'.

His impatience is such, he says, that he wants everything 'yesterday'.

He always regarded himself more as a stage than a film
actor. When he arrived in Hollywood first, he said: 'If
someone said ten years ago I'd be on a soundstage
here I would have told him he belonged on a funny
farm.'

He once said he could never understand why Joe Louis
was World Champion when, as everyone knew,
'Humphrey Bogart was the toughest guy in the world.'

George C Scott said of him, 'He's the best English
actor we have today. The mantle of Olivier will rest on
him if he doesn't get too commercial.'

He doubts that will happen. He doesn't want to end up
like some British stars in Hollywood, 'who sit around the
pool all day until their teeth fall out. Then they get
capped teeth and face jobs and end up in comedy series.'

The Sheens

Martin's real name is Ramon Estevez. Martin Sheen is a hybrid: Martin being in honour of a casting director at CBS called Robert Martin (who encouraged him to become an actor), and Sheen coming from Bishop Fulton Sheen. (He still uses Ramon Estevez on official documents such as his driving licence.)

He's the seventh son of ten children, nine boys and a girl. The family of twelve lived in a three-bedroomed house.

His left arm is three inches shorter than his right, because it was smashed by a forceps during his birth.

Charlie's real name is Carlos Irwin Estevez. 'He came into the world screaming,' says his father, 'and he hasn't stopped since.'

Emilio chose the surname Estevez because Emilio Sheen sounds stupid. He's the youngest writer-cum-actor-cum-director in film history.

When he was six he was mugged by a knife-wielding twelve-year-old in the lobby of his father's apartment. The robber got precisely 26 cents, which was how much he had saved up to pay for a hot-dog and a cream soda from the street vendor down the block.

Martin was so poor as a struggling actor that, instead of leaving *out* garbage on garbage night, he'd *collect* it. During a row about money, Martin's wife tore up $70 – and he spent the rest of the day taping it back together.

☆
☆ During the same period of his life he had a job clean-
☆ ing toilets with Al Pacino.

It's his voice you hear on the TV when Michael J Fox crawls out a window to fetch a Diet Pepsi for his pretty neighbour.

Emilio says he's seen *Jaws* seventy times.

Martin says he and his wife (Janet) have never agreed on anything in their entire lives.

He withdrew his name from the Academy's list of nominees for Best Actor after *Apocalypse Now*, because he doesn't believe actors should be in competition.

He says of acting: 'It's the most absurd thing in the world you can do. You always have to remember that 700 million people in China will never know who you are.'

'James Dean,' he says, 'was the strongest influence on any actor that ever stepped in front of a camera. Ever.'

He delivered his second son himself . . . 'and I was so stupid I thought the placenta was his twin!'

When his daughter Renee was missing on a beach once, he was about to dive into the surf to look for her, even though he can't swim a stroke. 'I knew if I tried to save her I'd most likely die,' he said afterwards, 'but I also knew that if I didn't try, I'd die too.'

Kevin Costner

He was so shy in his youth, he said he only had one date through all of High School. 'I was always the observer,' he says, 'and still am.'

He didn't start acting until he was twenty-two. He describes the early days thus: 'I'd walk out of offices with my fingers in my ears so I wouldn't hear someone who didn't know as much as I did telling me what to do.'

When he graduated from school he built a canoe and went on an expedition to the Indian Ocean.

He opted for acting against all the odds. 'If I had to get a job taking the trash out,' he said, 'it was gonna be Hollywood trash.'

His role in *The Big Chill*, which he felt would be his break-through movie, was reduced to some cameo shots and an appearance as a corpse being dressed by an undertaker. 'I have a kind of quiet career,' he said at the time. And afterwards, equally bemused, 'I could get cut out of a million movies, but getting cut out of a million-dollar hit, that was *something*.'

To learn how to use a gun in *The Untouchables*, the film that finally made his name, he took lessons from an eighty-eight-year old.

He doesn't go in for the trappings of success, driving a 1968 Mustang and shunning the party scene and drunken brawls. 'My lawnmower doesn't start when I want it to', he tells us, 'and the hoover jams up.'

☆ Not many people know he sings – or that he's had a
☆ Number One chart hit in Japan with his rock band
☆ Roving Boy.

His wife Cindy was a former Snow White at
Disneyland.

He describes acting as a 'holy' profession in which 'I
don't get caught lying very often'. But, he says, 'eighty
per cent of it is the ride there, the people you meet
along the way'.

Mel Gibson

He got the part of Mad Max, the film that made his name, through a freak occurrence. He had been beaten up a few days before the audition and his roughed-up appearance was what the casting unit were looking for.

He describes that film now as the 'classiest B-grade trash ever made'.

Prior to the shooting of *The Bounty*, he had a psychiatrist analyze the character of Fletcher Christian. 'I'll be playing him as the manic depressive paranoid schizophrenic he really was,' he said afterwards. He also wanted to hint at a possible homosexual liaison between Christian and Bligh.

He was more nervous presenting the Oscars in 1984 than in any film role, 'because I had no character to hide behind'.

He once described feminism, rather charmingly, as a term invented by some woman who got jilted.

He likes Sydney, Australia, because you can scream and wander around the backyard singing opera in your underpants if you want and nobody will think you're eccentric.

Of his fencing days he says, 'I loved plotting out the dirtiest, most violent ways of stabbing people.'

An actress he broke off a romance with in the mid-70s tried to slash her wrists at one of his parties.

☆ During the making of *Gallipoli* his life was threatened
☆ by funnel web spiders whose poison attacks the ner-
☆ vous system and then clots the blood.

When asked why he chose acting as a career he replied, 'I've been goofing round all my life. I thought I might as well get paid for it.'

When he took on the role of *Hamlet*, he got hate mail from his erstwhile fans, who called him a 'poofter bastard'.

Hamlet isn't the only theatrical role he's attempted; he played Estragon some years ago in *Waiting for Godot*. 'I was sixty years too young for that part,' he says rather mysteriously, 'but we used that.'

He's travelling so much these days, he says, he has to look at his passport to find out what country he's in.

Michael Douglas

He met his wife Diandra Luker when in the company of Jack Nicholson at a Jimmy Carter gala in 1977: 'Across a crowded room I saw her in a white dress, looking like a Botticelli madonna. I took her to the inauguration, it rained, and we went back to the hotel room. Eight weeks later we were married.'

The only thing that men and women have in common, he believes, is that they both like the company of men!

His father (Kirk) once said, 'If I knew he was going to be that successful, I would have been nicer to him as a kid.' He also said: 'Michael never had the advantages I had in life – he wasn't born poor.' And: 'Five minutes into watching *Wall Street*, I forgot Gordon Gekko was my son.'

After he made *The China Syndrome*, he says, 'I was getting sent every morose, sicko, wacko, diseased script. Cancer, poison, you name it – they all came down the tubes. If it's off-the-wall, send it to Mikey!'

He believes he's finally figured out the censor's ratings: 'PG means the hero gets the girl, Under 15s means the villain gets the girl . . . and Under 18s means *everyone* gets the girl.'

He was paid $10 million for *Basic Instinct*, a movie touted to make *Fatal Attraction* look tame – at least from the point of view of the sex scenes. But they're all choreographed, he says: 'It's like dance steps, or a fight

☆ scene. When she scratches your back, you have to arch
☆ two beats, then roll over, boom.'
☆

That movie outraged the homosexual community
because the villain was gay. Says Douglas, 'I've always
supported Gay Rights, but the whole thing of being
politically correct is a bore. In movies, somebody's got
to be the bad guy – and it can't *always* be the Italians.'

Lauren Bacall

She was born Betty Joan Perske in 1924, the same year Humphrey Bogart got married for the first time. (He would be married three times before she graduated from High School.)

Howard Hawks said of her liaison with Bogie: 'He fell in love with the character she played in *To Have and Have Not* – and she had to keep playing it for the rest of her life.'

'Okay,' she says, 'so a woman isn't complete without a man. But where do you find a man – I mean a *real* man – these days?'

She described life before she became famous thus: 'I used to come home from pounding the pavements, turn on a sad symphony to make me even lower, and sit there talking to a dog with big sad eyes.'

Of her singing in *The Big Sleep*, *Time* magazine wrote: 'She growls a *louche* song more suggestively than anyone in cinema has dared since Mae West in *She Done Him Wrong*'. In actual fact she only mouthed the words – the singing was done by Andy Williams.

She once gave sixty-two interviews in one week.

To Have and Have Not was such a success, playwright Moss Hart told her, 'You'd better retire right now. You'll never top the reviews you got for that.'

☆ After her sexually suggestive scene with Bogie in *To*
☆ *Have and Have Not*, she was liberally dubbed 'The
☆ Look' by the fanzines. But she was later to insist that
'The Look' itself was an accident: 'I was so nervous
that I held my head down hoping people wouldn't
notice I was shaking, and then I raised my eyes but not
my face when they spoke to me.'

She had her first child by Bogart when he was forty-
nine. He was on hormone treatment which caused all
of his hair (except for one sideburn and one eyebrow)
to fall out.

Not telling him he was dying of cancer was, she says,
her most flawless performance.

On the morning of 13 January 1957, after having been
in considerable pain for some hours he said to her.
'Boy, I hope I never have another night like that
again.' He never did.

John Wayne
★

His real name was Marion Mitchell Morrison.

Between 1948 and 1953 he made fifteen films . . . and 153 overall in his career.

His original ambition was to be a lawyer.

He always considered film-making a job rather than an art. 'I don't act,' he said once, 'I *re*-act.'

In the 30s he appeared in a number of B-westerns as a crooning cowpoke named Singin' Sandy.

For a cameo role in *The Longest Day*, he earned $250,000.

During a tobacco addiction spanning four decades, he rarely consumed fewer than four packs of cigarettes a day. When diagnosed as having lung cancer in the 60s, his intake was five packs daily of high tar, high nicotine brand; a chainsmoker by nature, he only used one match a day for his first cigarette, lighting the rest off each other.

When he was awarded an Oscar for playing Rooster Cogburn in *True Grit*, he commented: 'Wow, if I'd have known that, I'd have put on the eye-patch thirty-five years ago.'

In a 1978 operation he had a heart valve replaced with one from the heart of a pig. 'Make sure I don't have a curly tail when they bring me out of surgery,' he quipped.

☆ He was inordinately superstitious. If he was playing
☆ poker and a card turned face up by accident, he made
☆ its owner stand up and circle the table three times.

'Nobody liked my acting,' he once said, 'except the public.'

Asked once if President Nixon, a friend of his, had ever given him suggestions for his movies, he replied, 'No, they've all been successful.'

He claimed he couldn't hit a barn door with a six-gun in real life. 'But I can twirl one, which is just as good.'

A university student asked him once if he looked at himself as the fulfilment of the American Dream and he replied, 'Fella, I don't look at myself any more than I have to.'

In his last movie, *The Shootist*, he played a gun-fighter dying of cancer, which he was himself, in reality.

Of his latterday (more cossetted) co-stars he said: 'Some of them bitch about their hotel rooms . . . When I started in this business we slept in *tents*.'

His philosophy of acting was: 'Talk low, talk slow – and don't talk too damn much.'

When he was found to have a defective mitral valve in his heart one time, a doctor ruled out surgery because the risk factor of a major operation would be too great. Wayne threatened to jump out of a hospital window if the operation wasn't performed, saying: 'Measure your risk factor for that!' He got his way.

☆
☆
☆

'I'm a witch-hunter and a red-baiter,' he once boasted, 'and I've read 150 books on communism.'

When he was wracked with pain from the cancer which eventually killed him he asked his secretary-cum-lover Pat Stacy to get him his rifle so he could blow his brains out. She refused.

His grave is unmarked to this day; fans who visit his cemetery must leave flowers at the flagpole as attendants are ordered not to give any more details of where he's buried.

The 'Duke' sobriquet came from his dog.

Long-haired people, he once said, didn't bother him. 'But if a guy has his hair down to his ass I don't look at him and say, 'Now there's a fella I'd like to spend next winter with.'

He believed women have a right 'to work wherever they want to – so long as they have dinner ready when you get home'.

After marrying for the third time, he resigned himself to the fact that he would never understand women.

The day after he won his Oscar for *True Grit*, forty fellow actors greeted him on the set of another movie (*Rio Lobo*) all wearing eye-patches. And they put one on his horse as well.

During his second operation for cancer, two photographers dressed up as doctors to try to get a photograph of him on the operating table.

'I don't belong to any church,' he once said. 'If anything, I guess I'm a Presby-goddam-terian.'

Kirk Douglas

His real name is Issur Danielovitch.

His father was a ragman who bought old pieces of metal for junk and sold them from his wagon. He was born in Moscow but fled Russia in 1908 to escape being drafted into the Army.

When he was eight he was rescued from drowning after falling into a trench.

His father threw him through a door once when he flicked a teaspoon at him.

When he was twelve he played a shoe-maker in a school play and his father gave him an ice-cream cone afterwards. 'No award I have ever received has meant more to me than that cone,' he said years later.

He never heard his father call his mother by her name. Instead he'd say, 'Hey you!'

His father cried when he saw Kirk Douglas bleeding in a movie . . . but never when Issur Danielovitch shed *real* blood.

When he called on Gene Tierney he wasn't allowed to ring the doorbell: she would leave her bedroom window open and he had to climb up.

After his performance in *Champion* made him an
overnight star, gossip columnist Hedda Hopper said to
him, 'Now you've got a big hit you've become a real
son of a bitch.' 'I was always a son of a bitch,' he
replied. 'You just never noticed it before.'

After he appeared in *Ulysses*, a Russian radio station
said, 'Mr Douglas was so impressed with the script he
asked if Mr Homer had written any other ones.'

John Wayne once said he couldn't get on a horse without using a trampoline.

If people stay too late at his parties, 'I just put my pajamas on.'

His wife always cops it if he tries to lie to her: she says
he's the worst actor she knows.

He spent twenty-five years working on his autobiography, *The Ragman's Son*.

His helicopter collided with a plane in California in
1992 and – miraculously – he survived. 'I didn't think it
was time for me to go,' he said, 'I still have one more
chapter to write of my new book.'

He wears a pacemaker and, on this account, he's
decided he wants to be cremated when he dies. 'I can't
stand the idea of my corpse lying underground, with a
machine sending little electrical impulses to my dead
heart for years until the battery ran down.'

Sophia Loren

Sex, she said once, is like washing the dishes: 'You do it because you have to.'

She describes herself as 'a witch, with an acute extra-sensory perception, eerie premonitions and haunting superstitions.' Never a day of her life goes by, she claims, 'but I wear red to keep the demons at bay'.

'Any woman who swears she hasn't been made love to,' she says, 'has a right to swear.'

She was so thin as a child she was nicknamed Toothpick. Her mother's landlady advised her to let her die as she was only a drain on her finances and probably wouldn't live long anyway.

She met Carlo Ponti when she was fifteen and began living with him when she was nineteen. He was twenty-two years older than her, and married. The Vatican refused to allow him to marry her, which meant many court appearances on charges of bigamy (for him) and being a concubine (for her). Her mother's advice was; 'Wait around for him and you'll wind up an old maid lighting candles.'

She gave up playing the piano because her mother banged her on the head every time she made a mistake and the headaches finally became too bad.

She once described an unhappy childhood 'as a treasure you carry with you all your life'.

On the same day as she was branded a tax criminal in

Italy, she was presented to the Queen of England for a royal performance of one of her films.

☆
☆
☆

When she told a German magazine she hadn't received so much as a pair of shoes from her father in youth, he sued her for libel.

Time magazine once said that she could have swallowed most of her Hollywood leading men with half a glass of water.

When her grandmother died, she believes her spirit entered her body.

A fugitive from an asylum once attacked her with an axe, claiming that she was his lover. (She had given him an autograph some years before.)

After she became involved with Carlo Ponti, The Italian Men's Catholic Action Organisation demanded all Catholics boycott her films, but exhorted them to pray for her soul instead. One magazine suggested that if she had been living in the Middle Ages she would have been burned at the stake.

Noel Coward said of her, 'She should have been sculpted in chocolate truffles so the world could have devoured her.'

When she shared a plane with Bono once and became frightened of the thunder and lightning, he calmed her by saying, 'Don't worry; that's just God taking your photograph.'

She didn't get on with Marlon Brando during the filming of *The Countess from Hong Kong*. During one scene he said to her, 'Did you know you had hairs up your nostrils?'

☆ She met her brother for the first time at her father's
☆ deathbed. Her mother's reaction to the death was
☆ uncompromising; 'I hated him while he was alive
because he was a bastard; how does his dying affect
that?'

She was once invited to a gala charity ball in Brussels
but refused to go because she had a premonition about
it. The girl who replaced her, a former Miss Italy, was
killed in a plane crash on her return.

The two most important things in a relationship, she
feels, are 'red roses and white lies'.

Regarding her legendary voluptuousness, she comments: 'Everything you see I owe to spaghetti.'

Errol Flynn

He was descended on his mother's side from Fletcher Christian, and on his father's from a poor immigrant Irish family.

His father spent much of his life away on marine expeditions, his mother bringing a constant stream of men to the house in his absence.

He was dismissed from three schools for stealing, and a fourth for making love to a girl in a coalpile.

He was cruel to animals. He once glued a dog's eyelids together, and on another occasion clipped a parrot's wings, making it dance on a hot metal tub afterwards. He also liked putting snails on slime and watching them explode.

He was a spy for the Nazis during the Second World War.

He once estimated he spent between 12,000 and 14,000 nights making love.

He believed he was a pirate in a previous life.

He suffered from sinusitis, emphysema, gonorrhoea, a heart murmur and tuberculosis.

He once said of acting, 'There's no secret to the mastery of this art. Unlike other professions, seamanship for instance, it requires a mere modicum of common sense – plus, if you have it handy, a little vitamin B-1 whiskey.'

☆ He said of Hollywood, 'It's a lovely place to live. It's
☆ comfortable, it's warm and sunny. But it's filled with
☆ the most unutterable bastards.'

In 1942 he was charged on two separate cases of statutory rape.

His first film role was as a corpse.

He believed that anyone who died with more than £10,000 in his pocket was a failure.

Two people wrote him anonymous letters threatening his life if he didn't pay them money. One was a refugee from a mental institution, the other a thirteen-year-old boy. Neither was charged.

He was bisexual, spending nights with people like Truman Capote and Howard Hughes, and having a longer affair with Tyrone Power.

His wife had to pin him down sometimes to stop him reaching for a needle when he became addicted to morphine.

He brought his son to a brothel once to help him lose his virginity.

He sued *Confidential* magazine for alleging that he left his bride on his wedding night to visit a call girl.

Sometime he was so drunk on film sets he wasn't able to stand up. He would squirt oranges full of vodka with a hypodermic syringe and then suck them.

A safety deposit box in Switzerland which had con- ☆
tained $500,000 and other personal effects was found ☆
to be empty after his death. To this day nobody knows ☆
who opened it.

Some months after he died, his friend Ida Lupino
claimed he appeared to her and told her her mother
would die soon. Later that night she picked up the
phone to hear the news that her mother was smashed
to pieces in a car crash.

His son Sean disappeared in Vietnam in 1970 and
hasn't been heard of since.

Marilyn Monroe

She was born Norma Jeane Mortenson in 1926, the daughter of a woman who would spend the majority of her life institutionalized for paranoid schizophrenia. 'My mother didn't want me,' she said later, 'I must have disgraced her.'

She was unsure of the identity of her father right through her life.

She was made a ward of the county of Los Angeles early in life, being farmed out by the county welfare agency to a series of foster parents who were paid $20 a month to look after her.

At one of these she was seduced by an elderly boarder who gave her a nickel not to tell. When she did eventually tell she was punished for making up lies about a fine old man.

Tony Curtis likened kissing her in *Some Like It Hot* to kissing Hitler.

In 1962 she told an interviewer that Bobby Kennedy promised to marry her.

Asked what she wore on her wedding night she said, 'Chanel No 5.'

Constance Bennett complimented her thus: 'There goes a broad with a great future behind her.'

Nunnally Johnson claimed that talking to her was like trying to communicate with someone under water.

Laurence Olivier once said to her apropos her legendary unpunctuality: 'Why can't you be on time, for fuck's sake?' And she replied, unfazed: 'Oh, do you have that word in England too?'

As far as Jack Paar was concerned, 'She spoke in a breathless way that suggested either passion or asthma.' And wore necklines so low, it looked as though she'd jumped into her dress and caught her feet on the shoulder straps!

Billy Wilder said directing her was like directing Lassie: it took fourteen takes to get the bark right. Hollywood didn't destroy Marilyn Monroe, he believed, 'but it's the Marilyn Monroes who are destroying Hollywood.' She had, he said, 'breasts like granite, and a brain like Swiss cheese – full of holes'.

A smart girl, she once said, is one who knew how to play golf, tennis and the piano – and dumb.

When she was having her appendix out, she taped a note for the surgeon onto her abdomen. It read: 'Please take only what you have to. And please, please – no major scars.'

The first time a child asked her for her autograph, she had to ask the person standing next to her how to spell her Christian name.

After she secured her first major contract she was heard to say: 'Well at least that's the last cock I have to suck.'

She wasn't a fan of suntans because 'I like to feel blonde all over'.

Bob Hoskins

Many friends from his youth went into crime and he once contemplated that lifestyle for himself. 'Everyone said I was going to end up on the gallows,' he once commented.

He had an early job as a fire-eater in a circus, and described it thus: 'You fill your mouth with kerosene. Just keep the flames moving. You get used to it. The taste isn't very nice and you get indigestion now and again.'

He once played Iago and said afterwards, 'When you have to play a psychopath like that and you find you can do it, it's a bit worrying.'

He's won numerous acting awards but says he doesn't know what value they hold: 'Usually all an award means is that you don't work for eighteen months because nobody thinks they can afford you.'

When he was nominated for a Hollywood Oscar (for *Mona Lisa*) he said, 'I'm going to stay in the best hotel I can find. I'm going to drive to the Awards in the longest limousine I can find. I'm going to do everything in the worst possible taste. I'll be so gross you won't believe it.'

He got £130,000 from Francis Ford Coppola for being the stand-by to play Al Capone in *The Untouchables* if Robert de Niro wasn't available. He said to Coppola afterwards, 'If there's any other parts you don't want me to play, let me know.'

Of his role in *A Prayer for the Dying* he said, 'My old ☆
man's a socialist, I was brought up an atheist, and here ☆
I am playing a Catholic priest.' ☆

In just twelve days in America, *Roger Rabbit* took $37
million. (It grossed $150 million by the end of 1988.)
He said of his role here, 'A lot of actors boast about
appearing with Olivier or Gielgud but I was on film
with some of the *real* big guys – Bugs Bunny and
Mickey Mouse.'

'I love being famous,' he said once. 'All that pressure of
fame business is a load of bollocks.'

He got a late-night phone call in the summer of 1983
and a voice said, 'This is Francis Ford Coppola and I
want you to do a movie of mine.' He thought it was a
hoax so he said, 'Oh really. Well I'm Henry VIII and
you've just woken up my kid.'

'Marriage is definitely better the second time around,'
says the divorcé, adding, 'My first marriage didn't put
me off women – just women like my first wife.'

A colleague calls him every middle-class woman's idea
of a bit of rough trade. He doesn't see himself as a
womanizer, though. 'If I saw an eccentric old bugger
and a beautiful young girl sitting on a park bench,' he
once said, 'chances are I'd talk to the old geezer.'

Neither does he imagine himself to be the stuff that
movie stars are made of: 'You've got to be a bit glamorous for that. I'm 5 foot 6 inches and cubic.' He
believes he was well-cast as Mussolini, a shortsighted,
bald little cube with a big mouth.

Britt Ekland

Her original ambition was to become a vet.

When she was married to Peter Sellers he suffered eight heart attacks in the space of two hours one night.

Sellers insisted she keep her clothes on whenever she was having a massage.

In 1967 he had her removed from an Italian hotel by his agent with the words, 'She is leaving Rome this instant. Our marriage is finished.' Thereafter he tore off his wedding ring and flattened it into the carpet with his shoe.

Rod Stewart once turned down the chance of jamming with Bob Dylan to be with her.

Stewart often wore her cotton panties on stage instead of his own trunks because they were invisible beneath his skintight trousers.

'If any truth existed of Scottish meanness,' she says in her autobiography, 'then Rod was its manifestation.' She claims he made her buy the groceries at the cheapest store in town, and spend hours mending and darning his stage costumes.

Apart from this failing, though, he was generally good to her. He went so far as to sack a roadie once for swearing in her presence.

At other times she watched the same roadies throw breakfast trays out of their hotel windows, rip telephone wires out of walls, take legs from beds, sprays from showers and de-fusing entire suites.

She married Peter Sellers ten days after meeting him.

'When I give myself to a man,' she said once, 'I am at his command; whatever he desires I will do.' She described sex as 'a man's supreme game; his own private and perennial Olympics. He must always be made to feel he is the dominant force, even if the woman dictates the state of play.' She later said, 'When I adore someone, it's like an obsession to the death.'

She amended an original statement of 'I don't sleep with married men' to: 'I don't sleep with *happily* married men.'

She once attended a Beverly Hills analyst every day for a month at $100 a session.

After her marriage with Stewart broke up she sued him for $12 million.

Of her last marriage (to the Stray Cats' drummer Jim McDonnell) – they divorced after nine years together – she said: 'You don't have to have sex every night and bounce off the walls. It's the very trivial things that add up. I liked the familiarity of two toothbrushes in the bathroom.'

She seems to have a penchant for aligning herself with men of radically differing ages. Lou Adler, the father of her son, was nine years older than her. Peter Sellers was seventeen years older, while her penultimate lover, Jim McDonell, was seventeen years her junior.

She once told Rod Stewart, 'If you screw another woman while you're with me, I'll chop off your balls.'

Tony Curtis

★

His real name is Bernie Schwartz.

He didn't learn English until the age of seven.

A childhood playmate charged him 10 cents for his first kiss.

One money-making gambit at which he excelled in youth was: leaping in front of trucks, lying motionless on the ground until the driver braked, recovering slightly . . . and then being given cab money to get to hospital.

His brother Julius was knocked down for real as a child, dying two days later.

His mother he describes as a child-abuser: 'She beat me unmercifully for no reason. She used to slap my face because I was such a good-looking boy.'

His stage debut was as the idiot son of a lighthouse keeper in *Thunder Rock*. He had his head shaved for the role, even though he had only two lines to speak. When his mother saw him she screamed with fright, and he fluffed the lines.

At a premiere once he gave his car keys to the door-man with the words, 'Keep the car.' Because he thought that was the 'chic' thing to do.

He was given away as a prize once in a Win Tony Curtis for a Weekend competition. Afterwards, he said

☆
☆
☆

the woman who won him was disappointed. She was hoping for the second prize – a new stove.

His early efforts in film weren't the stuff of legend. After Elvis arrived in Hollywood, one critic wrote: 'I've now found someone to replace Tony Curtis as the world's worst actor.'

An avowed keep-fit fanatic, the one muscle he never considered developing, he says, was his brain.

He wrote a novel called *Kid Andrew Jody and Julie Sparrow* in 1978. When it didn't garner good reviews or sell well, his agent told him to buy all the copies up himself – at a cost of $8,000 – to get it onto the best-seller lists. He didn't go this far, but when the paper-back edition came out, he promoted it by appearing in a TV ad where he was seen stepping out of a Rolls Royce and saying, 'Why don't you give a struggling actor a break?'

'There's a bit of the Boston Strangler in all of us,' he said after playing that schizoid killer in the movie of the same name.

The chief function of cinemas, he feels, is to provide a place where young men can kiss their girlfriends with-out the fear of parents intruding.

He felt he was appropriately cast as a swindler in the 1974 TV series *McCoy*, 'because anyone who survives twenty-three years in Hollywood must be a con man'.

When he made *Trapeze* with Gina Lollobrigida, he was thirty and she thirty-three. But, he says, 'five years later she was thirty-one. When I reached forty I read

☆
☆
☆

somewhere that she was twenty-seven. When I was forty-three she was still thirty-three.'

He admits he said kissing Marilyn Monroe was like kissing Hitler, but what he really meant was, 'Here was this beautifully endowed woman treating all men like shit. Why did I have to take that?' (One scene in *Some Like It Hot* necessitated forty-one takes before she got the three words, 'It's me, Sugar,' right. Meanwhile, he nibbled forty-one chicken bones; he wasn't able to look at chicken for months afterward.)

He hasn't much time for ungrateful Hollywood children: 'Everyone's writing *Mommie Dearest* ... I'm going to write *Son and Daughter Dearest*.' (He is, of course, the father of Jamie Lee Curtis.)

He fell in love with English model Lesley Allen on the set of *The Boston Strangler* and proposed to her at his Hollywood mansion three months later. She refused because the said mansion didn't have an elevator. After he had one installed, she said yes. So they were married ...

Acting, he says, is ninety-five per cent research. Four per cent is turning up on time, getting along with the director and watching your diet. The other one per cent is talent.

The stunts on *Trapeze* were so dangerous, he says, 'even the doubles had doubles'!
Asked if he would ever like to appear on screen with his daughter Jamie Lee, he replied: 'Sure – I'd like to play her *mother*.'

A school chum said of him: 'He was Tony Curtis even before he was Bernie Schwartz.'

☆
☆
☆

During his heyday in films, he believed there was a small-print clause in all of his contracts specifying that he have affairs with all of his leading ladies.

He tells this story about the casting of *The Defiant Ones*: 'First they offered my part to Marlon Brando, but he wanted to play the black guy. Then they offered it to Kirk Douglas, but he wanted to play both parts. Finally they offered it to me, and I said okay, as long as I could do it in drag.'

The costume designer of *Some Like It Hot* said to Marilyn Monroe one day, 'Tony Curtis's ass is better-looking than yours.' To which she replied, 'Oh, yeah? Well he doesn't have tits like these!' as she yanked open her blouse.

A man who's had well-documented problems with alcohol and drugs, he once said, 'I spent twenty years reaching out for a glass or pill to make me feel good. Having a different woman all the time was part of the same dream. If a woman wasn't available, drugs eliminated the need for one.'

Basically, he describes himself as a man who doesn't want to grow up.

Marlene Dietrich

In 1932 she received a letter threatening to kidnap her daughter.

The war, she said, gave her the opportunity of kissing more soldiers than anyone else in the world.

In Las Vegas she once wore a gown that contained 227,000 hand-sewn beads which had taken six months to make. It was the result of a million stitches and was made from the breast feathers of 300 swans.

Alfred Hitchcock once said that, not only was she a professional actress, but a professional 'cameraman' (sic) to boot.

She was once spotted by a taxi driver at 3 am carrying a bundle of her child's washing from a laundry.

Her make-up man once said, 'This Dietrich has become the hardest kisser in movies; she needs a new mouth after every kiss.' (She once defined the relationship between a make-up man and an actress as one of accomplices in crime.)

At the height of her career she said, 'Acting just happens to be my profession. I could live very well without it. I have no ambition.'

Referring to Hitler after the war she said, 'I sometimes wonder if I just might have been the one person in the world who could have prevented the war and saved millions of lives.'

She once reproached a cameraman thus: 'When you were filming *The Garden of Allah* you made me look gorgeous. Why aren't these shots so good?' And the cameraman answered, 'Well Marlene, I'm eight years older now!'

'I feel at my happiest,' said Ernest Hemingway, 'when I have written something I am sure is good and Marlene likes it.'

'When I talk to Orson Welles,' she said once, 'I feel like a plant that's been watered.'

Asked if she would ever retire, she replied: 'That depends on the applause.'

Those Quotable Quotes

We all remember, 'Play it, Sam', 'I Want to be Alone', 'You Dirty Rat', 'Tomorrow is Another Day' and 'Come Back, Shane', but memorable lines from the movies don't end there. Try the following for size:

You know the first thing I found out? Bad news sells, because good news is no news.
Kirk Douglas in *The Big Carnival*

He'll regret it to his dying day – if he ever lives that long.
Victor McLaglen in *The Quiet Man*

We were just playing a game called Photography. You turn off the light and see what develops.
Barry Coe in *Peyton Place*

I've had hangovers before, but this time even my hair hurts.
Rock Hudson in *Pillow Talk*

My religion? I'm a millionaire, my dear.
Robert Morley in *Major Barbara*

He just swallowed his pride. It'll take him a moment or two to digest it.
Patricia Neal in *The Hasty Heart*

☆ I can afford a blemish on my character, but not on my
☆ clothes.
☆ **Vincent Price in *Laura***

I feel as though somebody stepped on my tongue with
muddy feet.
W C Fields in *Never Give a Sucker an Even Break*

I always start drinking around noon – in case it gets
dark early.
Peggy Lee in *Pete Kelly's Blues*

I liked you 'cos I thought you had some feeling, but
when I found out you hadn't, I liked you even more.
Mae West in *Go West, Young Man*

Your idea of fidelity is not having more than one man
in bed at the same time.
Dirk Bogarde to Julie Christie in *Darling*

Don't think too hard, Robert. You might hurt yourself.
Victor Moore in *Make Way for Tomorrow*

That's quite a dress you almost have on.
Gene Kelly in *An American in Paris*

The only thing you don't do in your dressing-room is
dress.
Michael Caine to Maggie Smith in *California Suite*

Roses by other names

The three wives of American chat-show host, Johnny Carson, are named Joan, Joanne and Joanna.

Shirley MacLaine was called after Shirley Temple.

The Marx Brothers all took their Christian names from a comic strip called *Mager's Monks*.

Stewart Granger's real name was James Stewart. Walter Matthau's is Walter Matuschanskayasky. And Rudolph Valentino's was ... Rudolpho Alfonzo Raffaelo Pierre Filibert Guglielmi di Valentino d'Antonguolla.

Karl Malden's original *Christian* name was Malden, and Woody Allen's was Allen.

In his early vaudeville days, George Burns worked under the names Willie Delight, Captain Belts and Buddy Links.

Mariel Hemingway was named after a bay in Cuba.

Conway Twitty created his stage name by combining the names of towns in Arkansas and Texas.

☆ Carole Lombard's real name was Carol Jane Peters.
☆ The Lombard came from a shop sign saying Lombardi
☆ Pharmacy which she spotted one day when she was
    sipping coffee in New York.

Mickey Mouse was originally christened Mortimer
Mouse. Goofy was first known as Dippy Dawg. Bugs
Bunny was Happy Rabbit, and Tom, of Tom and Jerry,
was first called Jaspar.

Gordon Mills was the man responsible for changing
Raymond O'Sullivan into Gilbert O'Sullivan, Thomas
Jones Woodward into Tom Jones, and Arnold Dorsey
into Engelbert Humperdinck.

Dionne Warwicke added the 'e' to her last name,
Warren Beatty added a 't' to his, Barbra Streisand
dropped an 'a' from Barbara, Rita Hayworth added
the 'y' to her last name, and Audry Hepburn-Ruston
dropped her double-barrelled surname and added an
'e' to her christian name.

Movie mogul Sam Goldwyn was born Samuel
Goldfish. Jean Arthur was Gladys Georgianna
Greene, Fred Astaire was Frederick Austerlitz,
Brigitte Bardot was Camille Javal, Jack Benny was
Benjamin Kubelsky and Cyd Charisse was Tula
Finklea.

Many stars have dropped their first names and taken
on a middle one instead. Gregory Peck's real first
name is Eldred, Steve McQueen's was Terence, Clark
Gable's was William, Montgomery Clift's was Edward,
Kim Novak's was Marilyn and Zsa Zsa Gabor was
Sari.

To Hollywood buffs, Doris Day is better known as The Professional Virgin – as is Jean Harlow the Platinum Blonde, Bob Hope Ski-Nose, Jeanette McDonald The Iron Butterfly, Jimmy Durante The Schnozz, and Clara Bow the "It" girl.

The following changed their names after they became famous with good reason – their real names being in brackets: Tony Curtis (Bernard Schwartz), Bobby Darin (Walden Waldo Cassotto), Bo Derek (Cathleen Collins), Sandra Dee (Alexandra Zuck), Angie Dickinson (Angeline Brown), Diana Dors (Diana Fluck), W.C. Fields (William Claude Dukenfield), John Garfield (Julius Garfinkle), Cary Grant (Archibald Leach), Laurence Harvey (Larushka Skikne) and Mario Lanza (Alfredo Cocozza).

When Cloris Leachman was asked by a reporter if that was her real name, she replied, 'Of course it's my real name. Would anyone in their right mind ever change to Cloris Leachman?'

Former Jobs

☆ ☆ ☆

Danny de Vito	Janitor
Kirk Douglas	Car-park attendant
Clint Eastwood	Lumberjack
Tom Hanks	Bellhop
Rutger Hauer	Electrician
Burt Lancaster	Acrobat
Madonna	Waitress
Kim Novak	Fridge demonstrator
Michael Douglas	Petrol-pump attendant
Gregory Peck	Trucker
Michelle Pfeiffer	Check-out girl
Barbra Streisand	Cinema usherette
Willem Dafoe	Magazine-binder at *Penthouse*
Anthony Quinn	Janitor
Jane Russell	Chiropodist's assistant
Bruce Willis	Rollerskating waiter
Elvis Presley	Truck driver
Glenn Close	Singer
Marlon Brando	Ditch digger
Jack Palance	Professional boxer
Cary Grant	$5-a-day stilt walker at a Coney Island fairground
Charlton Heston	Nude model for Art Student league of New York, coffin polisher, bricklayer and milkman
Robert Redford	Sewer commissioner
Raquel Welch	Cocktail waitress

Ronald Reagan ....Lifeguard ☆
Sean Connery ....Male model ☆
Victor Borge ....Funeral organist ☆
Rock Hudson ....Postman and truck driver
Eddie Duchin ....Pharmacist
Alan Ladd ....Hot-dog seller
Mickey Rourke ....Pretzel salesman
Malcolm McDowell ....Coffee salesman
James Cagney . . .Dancer in female impersonator's act
Anthony Quinn ....Dress cutter, janitor and
fruit picker
Dean Martin ....Steelworker
Lee Marvin ....Septic tank cleaner
Stan Laurel ....Understudy to Charlie Chaplin
Walter Matthau ....Filing clerk
Alan Alda ....Clown, cabdriver and colourer
of baby photographs
Yul Brynner ....Acrobat
Charles Bronson ....Coalminer
Sylvester Stallone ....Trainee beautician
James Caan ....Rodeo rider
Glenn Ford ....Bus driver
Michael Caine ....Meat porter
Clark Gable ....Lumberjack and
telephone repairman
Sydney Greenstreet ....Tea planter in India
Rod Steiger ....Civil servant
Oliver Reed ....Bouncer in a strip club
James Cagney ....Waiter
W C Fields ....Juggler
Gary Cooper ....Stuntman
John Wayne ....Studio prop man and
professional footballer

Offers they *could* refuse

☆ ☆ ☆

David Niven turned down the role of Hopalong Cassidy.

Tuesday Weld refused lead roles in *Cactus Flower*, *True Grit*, *Bonnie and Clyde* and *Bob and Carol and Ted and Alice*.

Henry Fonda felt the leading role in *Network* was too hysterical for him; it netted Peter Finch a posthumous Oscar.

Julie Harris said no to playing Alma in *From Here To Eternity*. Donna Reed stepped in instead and also walked off with an Oscar.

The part of Nurse Ratchet was refused by Anne Bancroft, Coleen Dewhurst, Geraldine Page and Angela Lansbury before Louise Fletcher set the screen alight with her portrayal of that nefarious individual in *One Flew Over the Cuckoo's Nest*.

Judy Garland, Rita Hayworth and Eleanor Parker all refused to play Jean Harlow's mother in *Harlow* before Ginger Rogers took the part.

When Greta Garbo was offered the eponymous role in *The Country Girl*, she refused point blank, as did

Jennifer Jones (because she was pregnant); Grace Kelly took the role.

Angie Dickinson feels the worst career move she ever made was foregoing the chance to play Krystle in *Dynasty*.

Jacqueline Onassis was offered $1 million to play herself in *The Greek Tycoon*. She wasn't interested, and Jacqueline Bisset did it for half that.

As well as *The Graduate*, Robert Redford refused roles in *Rosemary's Baby*, *Who's Afraid of Virginia Woolf?*, *Love Story* and *The Day of the Jackal*.

Warren Beatty turned down *both* parts in *Butch Cassidy and the Sundance Kid*.

Before Michael Caine took *Alfie*, Anthony Newley, James Booth, Terence Stamp and Laurence Harvey were all offered the chance to play the cocky cockney.

Marlon Brando refused the role Frank Sinatra subsequently played in *The Man with the Golden Arm*. It revived Sinatra's flagging career.

Montgomery Clift turned down the lead role in *Sunset Boulevard* because he felt audiences wouldn't accept him playing love scenes with a woman thirty-five years his senior. The role became one of William Holden's most memorable.

Kirk Douglas turned down the part of Kid Sheleen in *Cat Ballou*, a part that won Lee Marvin an Oscar.

☆ Jane Fonda turned down an eponymous part in *Bonnie*
☆ *and Clyde*. The film made Faye Dunaway a star
☆ overnight.

Cary Grant refused the lead role in *Let's Make Love*
because he didn't want to play opposite Marilyn
Monroe.

Alan Ladd refused to play Jett Rink in *Giant*. He felt
he was too old. It turned out to be a hit for James
Dean, but was his last film.

Hedy Lamarr wouldn't star in *Casablanca* because it
was an unfinished script. Ingrid Bergman eventually
landed the role, thus inscribing herself in cinema memory for ever more.

Burt Lancaster turned down *Ben-Hur*, a role that won
an Oscar for Charlton Heston.

Eva Marie-Saint turned down a role in *The Three
Faces of Eve* that won an Oscar for Joanne Woodward.

Robert Redford refused to play *The Graduate* because
he felt he hadn't the naivety for the role. It made
Dustin Hoffman a household name.

George Raft wouldn't play Sam Spade in *The Maltese
Falcon* because he didn't like the idea of working with
its 'unknown' director: John Huston.

It's a wrap . . . or is it?

☆ ☆ ☆

The John Wayne movie *Stagecoach* was set in the nine-teenth century, but if you look carefully, you can see tyre tracks clearly visible in the desert sand during some of the scenes.

Rudoph Valentino wears a Cartier watch on his wrist during the major love scene in *The Sheik* . . . made in 1921.

In the Oscar-winning *It Happened One Night*, Clark Gable leaves his motel room at 2.30 am, drives around New York, writes a story for his newspaper and returns to his room . . . where the clock still reads 2.30 am.

In *Star Wars*, Carrie Fisher plays Princess Leia. At one point Mark Hamill greets her by her real name.

In *The Wrong Box*, which is set in Victorian times, you can see a number of TV aerials on the roofs of houses.

Janet Leigh gulps twice in *Psycho* when she's lying on the bathroom floor . . . dead.

During one scene in *Anatomy of a Murder*, Lee Remick is seated in a café wearing a snow-white dress; a couple of seconds later she emerges from it in a pair of trousers.

In Hitchcock's *North by Northwest*, Eva Marie Saint reaches into her purse to pull out a gun and shoot Cary

☆ Grant ... but before she does so, a boy sitting in the
☆ background puts his fingers in his ears. (He had heard
☆ the bang during rehearsals.)

In *Steel Magnolias*, Sally Field's two teenage sons
remain the same age – with the same hairstyles and set
of clothes – even though the movie covers a three-year
period.

Yul Brynner's earring in *The King and I* switches from
ear to ear – and sometimes vanishes altogether.

Sean Connery drives a Ford Mustang on its two right
wheels through a narrow alley in *Diamonds are
Forever*, but it emerges from the alley on its two *left*
wheels.

King Arthur wears a plaster on his neck in *Camelot*.

In Walt Disney's *The Story of Robin Hood*, Maid
Marian wears a dress with a zipper. More recently, the
Jesus of Martin Scorsese's *The Last Temptation of
Christ* wears a robe with double-seamed machine
stitches – and marks where a label had been attached.

In *Carrie*, a car in the background of one of the scenes
can be seen travelling backwards at 200 mph because
of a special effects blunder.

The 1969 movie titled *Krakatoa, East of Java* is geo-
graphically incorrect: Krakatoa is actually *west* of Java.

In the movie *Quicksilver*, Kevin Bacon cycles down a
New York street ... and turns the corner into San
Francisco!

In Alfred Hitchcock's *Rear Window*, James Stewart's
plaster cast moves from his left leg to his right one for
a whole scene.

During one scene in *The Untouchables*, a dead body
moves from one end of a room to the other on its own.

Cut!

Contrary to what you might believe, it's never roses all the way for film stars. Here are a few of the turkeys they would prefer to have bypassed – or forgotten.

I've never played anyone but myself on screen. No, I take that back. Once I tried to throw myself into the role of a Spanish gypsy. The picture was *The Loves of Carmen* with Rita Hayworth, and it was the biggest bomb in history.
Glenn Ford

The only film I ever made that I'm truly ashamed of was a Western called *Sea of Grass*. Spencer Tracy was supposed to be a cowboy born to the saddle, but he took one look at the horse and it hated him and the whole thing was a disaster.
Elia Kazan

I tried to break out of the Rocky mould with *Paradise Alley*. I'll never forget walking into a cinema on the opening day. There were about thirty people: you could have hunted f***ing *deer* in there.
Sylvester Stallone

Dean Martin was walking round the Fox lot one day and bumped into me while I was wearing full regalia for *Prince Valiant*, my worst bomb. Observing the

☆ black wig and bangs, he talked to me for ten minutes
☆ before he realized I wasn't Jane Wyman.
☆ **Robert Wagner**

After *The Freshman* I'm retiring. I wish it hadn't finished with a stinker.
Marlon Brando

Sincerely Yours was my big try for stardom on the screen,
but no one noticed it or me. Maybe I should have worn
my candelabra on my head, Carmen Miranda-style.
Liberace

Jimmy Cagney and I both reached the bottom with
The Bride Came C.O.D. He spent most of his time in
the picture removing cactus quills from my behind.
Bette Davis.

Two On a Guillotine wasn't a picture, it was an abor-
tion. The guillotine was put in the wrong place. They
should have cut off William Conrad's head for producing the thing.
Max Steiner

All I remember of *The Miracle* is leading a parade of
soldiers through the streets of Brussels in Rosalind
Russell's corset from *Auntie Mame*.
Roddy McDowell

I was once in a film called *Oh Dad, Poor Dad, Mama's
Hung You in the Closet and I'm Feelin' So Sad*. Need I
say more?'
Rosalind Russell

Bog was never finished. I was never paid. They
released it incomplete and then it disappeared, like a

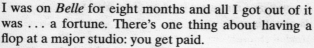

floating crap game. I have a copy of it. The monster looks like a huge chicken.
Gloria de Haven

☆
☆
☆

I was on *Belle* for eight months and all I got out of it was . . . a fortune. There's one thing about having a flop at a major studio: you get paid.
Fred Astaire

I was once inveigled into a remake of *The Awful Truth*, which was a fizzle of the worst kind. I still haven't been paid for it, and rightly so.
Ray Milland

Overboard was the biggest disappointment I've ever had. It's like having a big fish at the end of your line and then you bring it up and it just kind of wiggles off your hook.
Goldie Hawn

The failure of *Avalanche* and *Darling Lili*? Well one movie had a glacier and the other had Julie Andrews. I guess the audience couldn't tell the difference.
Rock Hudson

I must have had brain damage to get involved with *Convoy*.
Kris Kristofferson

I made a movie called *Quick, Before it Melts*. You had to catch it quick, before it disappeared.
George Maharis

I don't think John Ford ever liked *The Horse Soldiers*. One day we were sitting around on his boat and he said to me, 'You know where we ought to make this

☆ picture?' 'No,' I said, 'Where?' 'In Lourdes. It's going
☆ to take a miracle to pull it off.'
☆ **John Lee Mahin**

I never met anyone who saw *One Way Street*.
James Mason

When I made *The Horn Blows at Midnight* I made one
mistake – I put film in the camera.
Jack Warner

Noel Coward accompanied me to the preview of
Surprise Package. As we were leaving the theatre, a
lady came up to him and told him he stole the picture.
'It was petty larceny, my dear,' he replied, 'believe me.'
Stanley Donen

We released *Six Weeks* at Christmastime and never
stopped to consider that people wouldn't want to
spend the holidays going to films about a little girl having six weeks to live.
Dudley Moore

Joanne, my wife, read the script of *A New Kind of
Love* and thought it would be fun to do together. I told
her I thought it was just a bunch of one-liners and she
said, 'You son of a bitch. I've been carting your children round, taking care of them at the expense of my
career, taking care of you and your house.' And I said,
'I think it's a terrific script. I can't think of anything I'd
rather do.' This is what's known as a reciprocal trade
agreement.
Paul Newman

On *Scrooged* I was trapped on a dusty, smelly, smoky
set in Hollywood for three and a half months, having a

lousy time by myself, coughing up blood from this fake snow that was falling all the time.
Bill Murray

The Escape Artist played in theatres for two minutes before going into aeroplanes. You have to pay $500 to see it now.
Teri Garr

I made *Quicksand* for $10,000. As a few hundred critics wrote, I sank in the stuff.
Mickey Rooney

Audiences stayed away from *The Lady in Ermine* like it was *The Lady with Leprosy*. I thought, well there's one consolation, it can't get any worse than this. Then along came *The Beautiful Blonde from Bashful Bend*.
Betty Grable

I called my agent and said I needed some money, and do you know what they got for me? *The Swan*, where my big line was, 'The bees are coming.'
Lee Grant

Enter stage left

Actor Sidney Poitier only weighed 3lbs at birth.

Jack Lemmon was born in a hospital lift.

Victoria Principal was born in Japan. Audrey Hepburn began life in Belgium, Julie Christie in India, and Bianca Jagger in Nicaragua. Both Bob Hope and Liz Taylor were born in England.

Horror movie stars Vincent Price, Peter Cushing and Christopher Lee were all born on 27 May.

Warner Brothers changed James Cagney's birthdate from 1899 to 1904 to exploit his baby-faced appearance.

They changed Humphrey Bogart's birthdate from 23 January to Christmas Day to add glamour to his image.

Barbara Bel Geddes, who played JR Ewing's mother in *Dallas*, was born only nine years before him. Rod Steiger was born a year after Marlon Brando, yet played his older brother in *On the Waterfront*. Rosemary de Camp, who played James Cagney's mother in *Yankee Doodle Dandy*, was fourteen years younger than him.

Horror star, Bela Lugosi, who played Dracula many times on celluloid, was actually born in Transylvania.

Clark Gable was listed as a female on his birth certificate.

It's all relative

☆ ☆ ☆

Perry Como and Glen Campbell are both seventh sons of seventh sons.

Lon Chaney's parents were both deaf mutes.

It was Marlon Brando's mother who encouraged Henry Fonda to become an actor.

Sylvester Stallone's son is called Sage Moonblood.

Charlton Heston's son played his on-screen son in *The Ten Commandments*.

Elvis Presley's parents were extras in *Loving You*, – their first and last movie.

Nancy Reagan is the daughter of a New Jersey car salesman.

Both Marlon Brando's son (Christian) and Frank Sinatra's were kidnapped and returned safely – in 1972 and 1964 respectively.

The sons of Paul Newman, Gregory Peck and Mary Tyler Moore all committed suicide.

Sophia Loren's sister married Mussolini's son.

☆ Rita Hayworth was a first cousin of Ginger Rogers.

☆

☆ Olivia de Havilland and Joan Fontaine were sisters.

Mia Farrow's mother Maureen O'Sullivan played her on-screen mother in *Hannah and Her Sisters*.

Joan Plowright played Laurence Olivier's daughter in *The Entertainer*, though in real life they were married to one another.

James Arness and Montgomery Clift both had twin sisters.

Many Hollywood stars have had their lineage traced to one Lady Diana Spencer. Humphrey Bogart was her seventh cousin, twice removed. Olivia de Havilland was her fifth cousin, three times removed. Orson Welles was her eighth cousin, twice removed. Lee Remick was her tenth cousin, twice removed and Lillian Gish was her double seventh cousin, three times removed.

Angela Lansbury was only three years older than her son Laurence Harvey in *The Manchurian Candidate*.

Charles Bronson claimed his family were so poor, he started school in dresses that were hand-me-downs from his older sister.

John Barrymore was seduced by his stepmother at the age of fifteen.

Sylvester Stallone's father played a time-keeper in the first *Rocky* movie.

Jocelyn Brando appeared with her brother Marlon in *The Ugly American*.

Funny Money

☆ ☆ ☆

Liz Taylor was the first actress to command $1 million for a film, *Cleopatra*.

Larry Hagman got $75,000 per episode of *Dallas* as JR.

When Burt Reynolds posed nude in *Playboy* in 1972 a Chicago woman bought 500 copies of the magazine (at a cost of $700) to wallpaper her bedroom. 'For that,' said Burt, 'I would have come over and seen her myself.'

Child actress Drew Barrymore was paid a record $250,000 advance for her life story. (At fourteen, she was the youngest autobiographer of all time.)

David O Selznick was fined $5,000 for allowing the word 'damn' to be used in *Gone With the Wind*.

Hollywood producers offered Sylvester Stallone $360,000 for his *Rocky* script – but only $75,000 if he came with it. He took the latter option. (He received $19½ million for *Rambo 3*.)

The closing credits for *Star Trek* cost more than *Friday The 13th* and *Airplane* budgets combined!

The film *The Longest Day* cost more than the war on which it was based.

☆ After filming *The Graduate*, Dustin Hoffman collected
☆ unemployment benefit, though the film went on to
☆ gross over $50 million.

Warner Brothers paid $52,000 for Sean Connery's
hairpiece in *Never Say Never Again*.

The two lowest paid stars in *The Wizard of Oz* were
Judy Garland and the dog Toto.

The double bed used by Marilyn Monroe and Joe di
Maggio in their brief marriage fetched $25,000 at a
New Jersey auction in 1989.

Producer Adolf Zucker's 100th birthday party was
special because Paramount auctioned off all the candles on his cake for $1,000 each.

For the leading role in *The Lords of Flatbush*,
Sylvester Stallone said he received twenty-five free T-
shirts.

Michael Caine said his fee for Neil Jordan's critically
acclaimed *Mona Lisa* was 'two bob and a lollipop'.

Each time Johnny Carson's *Tonight Show* theme song
is played, Paul Anka – who wrote it – gets $200.

Howard Hughes spent $12 million trying to buy up
every copy of his flop *The Conqueror* . . . which cost
$6 million to make.

Cecil B de Mille spent $100,000 researching the real
colour of Egypt's pyramids so that his *Cleopatra* could
be authentic. The answer his aides came back with was
that they were precisely the colour the man in the
street always thought: sandy brown.

Marilyn Monroe received $50 for her famous nude calendar shot; it netted the calendar company in excess of $750,000.

Robert Taylor signed with MGM for $35 a week in 1934.

Kim Novak got $100 a week from Columbia for appearing in *The Man with the Golden Arm*, while her director, Otto Preminger, had to pay the studio that released her to do the movie for him $100,000.

Trevor Howard's most famous role, in *Brief Encounter*, netted him £500.

Karen Black's salary for *Can She Bake a Cherry Pie?* was $1,038, but since she made that movie without the Screen Actor's Guild's approval, that body fined her ... $1,038.

Montgomery Clift did his Oscar-winning cameo in *Judgment At Nuremberg* for nothing as a gesture towards persecuted Jews in Nazi Germany, though his agent had originally requested a six-figure sum for his services. After the movie was canned, Clift sent the agent a paper bag containing his commission: it was empty.

James Dean was paid $30 for his first professional acting job: a Pepsi commercial.

When James Stewart left acting to go into the Navy in the 40s, his monthly salary was a whopping $21. He forwarded his agent the fee of ten per cent (2 dollars and 10 cents), who duly framed it.

☆
☆ Peter Falk of *Columbo* fame bought his trademark
☆ trenchcoat for $20 in 1967 at a store in New York.

In the early 40s, Charlton Heston was a nude model
for the Art Student League in New York – at a rate of
$1.25 an hour.

Sex, Lies and Videotape

☆ ☆ ☆

If you think movie sex is anything but a four-letter word, sample the following quotes from those who've been there:

Suddenly you wind up in bed with a guy on top of you that you wouldn't want to share a cab with.
Candice Bergen

You've got to do acrobatics and contortions so the lighting and camera angles are right. Sorry, guys, but love scenes are work.
Michael Douglas

You say things you never thought of, surrounded by people you don't know, to a girl you've only met a few days before . . . I've been given love scenes to do that read like political speeches.
Marcello Mastroianni

In *Alfie*, when I was supposed to be on top of Michael Caine, I had little pillows placed all over his body so we wouldn't touch. He was screaming so much with laughter we almost didn't get the scene done.
Shelley Winters

We all have to start somewhere. Marilyn Monroe did it with that calendar, Lana Turner with a sweater. I had to go a little bit better.
Linda Lovelace on *Deep Throat*

☆ The word 'Cut!' is a very good cold shower.
☆ *Kathleen Turner*
☆

Darling, if I get excited during this scene, please forgive me. And if I *don't* get excited, please forgive me.
Tom Berenger to sometime co-star in bed scene

I may not be a great actress but I've become the greatest at screen orgasms – ten seconds heavy breathing, roll your head from side to side, simulate a slight asthma attack . . . and die a little.
Candice Bergen

Of course I fell in love with him. I mean, that's what it's about, isn't it?
Susan Sarandon on James Spader, co-star of *White Palace*

I hope my kissing doesn't look like I'm sucking paint off my car.
Charlie Sheen

Sex scenes are just, well, boring. Especially after filming the same scene for three days. You start to think, 'I'd like to hop into some pants again.'
Matt Dillon

I rushed out and slammed him against the wall, saying 'If you don't open your mouth I'm going to rape you.'
Kelly Lynch on Tom Cruise during the making of *Cocktail*

He was always self-conscious about his teeth. I hoped I wouldn't start laughing.
Laurie Hobbs on teaching Tom Cruise how to kiss

I'll bet each of these honeys is worth six, maybe seven million.
John Caglione on Madonna's breasts in *Dick Tracy*

Making love on screen is really the most sexless and boring thing in the world.
Joan Collins

☆
☆
☆

He was extremely nervous. I cracked jokes and it turned out I was the only one who hadn't done it in the back of a car before.
Sean Young on making love to Kevin Costner in *No Way Out*

Remember, this film is all about sex. Even if we're just standing across a room looking at each other.
Jack Nicholson to Jessica Lange on the set of *The Postman Always Rings Twice*

I was thinking, Oh God, please don't let nature takes its course.
Patrick Swayze on his love scenes with Demi Moore in *Ghost*

I like to be naked in movies. I have a reputation to uphold.
Alec Baldwin

If you see people kiss in the right way, it can make you as horny as seeing the lower regions doing it.
Tony Scott, director of *Top Gun*

It's intensely difficult and harrowing to do a love scene in front of all these people. I usually end up sobbing in the dressing-room after every take.
Kathleen Turner

I just opened my mouth and descended slowly from the top of the frame to Nola Darling's nipples.
Spike Lee on the opening to *She's Gotta Have It*

Robin has tremendous scars on his back from prison, but the camera never picked that up. It was just another opportunity to titillate.
Kevin Costner over-rating his *derrière* in the way they shot *Robin Hood: Prince of Thieves*

Eye Strain

Do you think Hollywood stars are vain about their appearances? Judge from the following quotations:

I've never liked my face. The left side's predatory.
Raquel Welch

If you lose weight to keep your ass, your face goes. But if the face is good, the ass isn't. I'll choose the face.
Kathleen Turner

I have the eyes of a dead pig.
Marlon Brando

If you haven't cried, your eyes can't be beautiful.
Sophia Loren

I'm perfect. The areas that I need help on aren't negotiable. They're to do with gravity.
Jane Fonda

Jane Fonda didn't get that terrific body from exercise. She got it from lifting all her money.
Joan Rivers

Blonde hair, pink lips, good figure, talent and sex. That's all I have to offer. It's paid off, too.
Diana Dors

I was never beautiful like Miss Hayworth or Miss Lamarr. I was known as the little brown wren. Who'd want me at the end of the picture?'
Bette Davis

It's really a joke that my whole life people thought I was unattractive until now – when I'm too old to be able to do much about it.
Cher

There's a lot of good-looking, well-built guys in this business and most of them couldn't play a corpse.
James Caan

A Kiss is Just a Kiss

Have you ever wondered what it would be like to kiss Tom Cruise on screen? Does the Pope pray?

But maybe it's not all it's cracked up to be. Here are a few reminiscences of those – male and female – who kissed and told. For better or worse.

There's an art to it. You have to convince yourself it's as good as what's coming later.
Kim Basinger

When Clark Gable kissed me they had to *carry* me off the set.
Carroll Baker

It becomes a bore. I prefer to fight.
Alain Delon

I'm fond of it. It's part of my job. God sent me down to earth to kiss a lot of people.
Carrie Fisher

I've been kissing Audrey Hepburn all day and my pucker is tuckered.
James Garner

When I was in pictures, you had a time limit of two seconds before cutting away to a curtain blowing – and

you couldn't open your mouth. If you had a sinus you'd just die.
John Derek

Before we shot the kissing scene in *The Front*, Woody Allen said, 'I'm going to give you only one lip because if I gave you two you'd never live through it.'
Andrea Marcovicci

Index of Hollywood Stars

☆ ☆ ☆